Pamphlets. Translated From the Russian

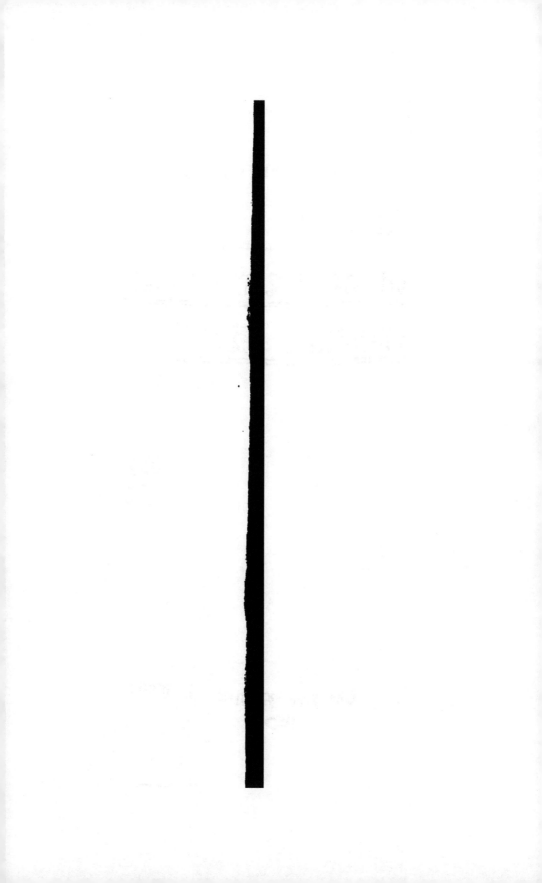

THREEPENCE

Letters to Friend

on the Personal

Christian Life.

By L
Colst

The Free Age Press
1900

The Free Age Press stands for an
attempt to assist in spreading those deep convictions in which the noblest spirits of every age
and race have united—that man's true aim and
happiness is "unity in reason and love"; the
realisation of the brotherhood of all men,—and
that we *must* all strive to purge away, each from
himself, those false ideas, false feelings, and false
desires, personal, social, religious, political, racial,
economic, which alienate us one from another and
produce nine-tenths of the sum of human suffering.

Of these truly Christian and universally religious
aspirations the writings of Leo Tolstoy are perhaps
to-day the most definite expression, and it is to
the production of 1d., 3d., and 6d. editions of
all his known religious, social, and ethical works,
together with the unpublished matter and future
writings to which we have and shall have special
access (being in close relationship with Tolstoy),
that *The Free Age Press* will at first devote itself;
trusting that all who sympathise will assist by
every means in their power, especially in helping
to spread the books the world over, losing no
opportunity of introducing them whenever and
wherever feasible, and of so making it possible
for the work to be continued, and extended into
wider and wider fields. As it is Tolstoy's desire
that his books shall not be copyrighted, our editions will, whenever possible, be free to the world.

Suggestions, criticisms, inquiries, offers of help
and co-operation will be gratefully welcomed;
and it is specially requested that the names of any
books that have helped towards a better understanding of life may be furnished, so that a much
needed list may be compiled and published.

Letters, Private Orders, and Money Orders (it
is hoped that friends will *purchase* as many copies
as possible: even one will help) should be ad-
dressed to THE EDITORS, "FREE AGE PRESS,"
MALDON, ESSEX. *Booksellers* must order from
Messrs. SIMPKIN, MARSHALL, HAMILTON, KENT,
& Co. LTD., London, E.C.; THE CLARION Co.,
LTD., 72 Fleet Street, E.C.; Messrs. JOHN
MENZIES & Co., Glasgow; and Mr. JOHN
HEYWOOD, Manchester.

LETTERS TO FRIENDS
ON THE PERSONAL
CHRISTIAN LIFE

UNIFORM WITH

"ON THE PERSONAL CHRISTIAN LIFE."

Long 8vo, sewed, 3d. each ; post free, 3½d.

PATRIOTISM AND GOVERNMENT. LEO
TOLSTOY.

THOUGHTS ON GOD. LEO TOLSTOY.

LETTERS ON WAR. LEO TOLSTOY.

SOME SOCIAL REMEDIES (Socialism,
Anarchy, Communal Life, Land Nationalisation, etc.). LEO TOLSTOY.

RELIGION AND MORALITY. LEO TOL-
STOY.

———

IN PREPARATION.

THE RELATION OF THE SEXES. LEO
TOLSTOY.

EDUCATION OF CHILDREN. LEO TOL-
STOY.

CONCEPTIONS OF LIFE. LEO TOLSTOY.

CHRISTIAN ANARCHY. LEO TOLSTOY.

LETTERS TO . .
FRIENDS ON . .
THE PERSONAL .
CHRISTIAN LIFE

By LEO .
TOLSTOY

THE FREE AGE PRESS
CHRISTCHURCH, HANTS . .
(New Address)

1900

7-3-62

LETTERS TO FRIENDS

ON THE

PERSONAL CHRISTIAN LIFE

———◆———

To E. H. C.

(Translation by Aylmer Maude.)

DEAR MR. ——,—I am very glad to
have news of your activity, and to
hear that your work begins to attract
attention. Fifty years ago Lloyd Garrison's Declaration of Non-resistance
only estranged people from him; and
Ballou's fifty years' labour in the same
direction was constantly met by a con-
spiracy of silence. I now read with
great pleasure in the *Voice* admirable
thoughts by American writers on this
question of Non-resistance. I need
only demur at the notion expressed by
Mr. B. It is an old but unfounded
libel upon Christ to suppose that the
expulsion of the cattle from the temple
indicates that Jesus beat people with

a whip and advised His disciples to behave in a like manner.

The opinions expressed by these writers, especially by H. N. and G. D. H., are quite correct, but unfortunately they do not reply to the question Christ put to men, but to another question, which has been substituted for it by those chief and most dangerous opponents of Christianity—the so-called "orthodox" ecclesiastical authorities.

Mr. H. says, "I do not believe Non-resistance admissible as a universal rule." H. N. says "that people's opinion as to the practical results of the application of Christ's teaching will depend on the extent of people's belief in his authority." C. M. considers "the transition stage in which we live not suited for the application of the doctrine of Non-resistance." G. D. H. holds "that to obey the law of Non-resistance we must learn how to apply it to life." Mrs. L., thinking that the law of Non-resistance can be fully obeyed only in the future, says the same.

All these views refer to the question, What would happen if people were all obliged to obey the law of Non-resistance? But, in the first place, it is impossible to oblige every one to accept this law. Secondly, if it were possible to do so, such compulsion would in itself be a direct negation of the very principle set up. Oblige all men to refrain ` from violence ! Who then should enforce the decision ? Thirdly, and this is the chief point, the question as put by Christ is not at all, Can Non-resistance become a general law for humanity ? but, How must each man act to fulfil his allotted task, to save his soul, and to do the will of God ?—which are all really one and the same thing.

Christian teaching does not lay down laws for everybody, and does not say to people, " You, all, for fear of punishment, must obey such and such rules, and then you will all be happy "; but it explains to each individual his position in relation to the world, and lets him see what results, for him individually, inevitably flow from that relation. Christianity says to man (and to each man separately) that his personal life can have no rational meaning if he counts it as belonging to himself, or as having for its aim worldly happiness for himself or for other people. This is so because the hap-

piness he seeks is unattainable: (1)
for as all beings strive after worldly
advantages, the gain of one is the
loss of others; and it is most probable
that each individual will incur much
superfluous suffering in the course of
his vain efforts to seize unattainable
blessing; (2) because even if a man
gets worldly advantages, the more he
obtains the less they satisfy him, and
the more he hankers after fresh ones;
(3) and chiefly because the longer a
man lives, the more inevitable becomes
the approach of old age, sickness, and
of death, destroying all possibility of
worldly advantages.

So that if man considers his life his
own, to be spent in seeking worldly
happiness for himself as well as for
others, then that life can have no
rational explanation for him.

Life has a rational meaning only
when one understands that to consider our life our own, or to see its aim
in worldly happiness for ourselves or
for other people—is a delusion; that a
man's life does not belong to him who
has received it, but to Him who has
given it, and therefore its object should
be not the attainment of worldly
happiness either for one's self or for

other individuals, but solely to fulfil the will of Him who created this life.

This conception alone gives life a rational meaning, and makes its aim (which is to fulfil the will of God) attainable. And, most important of all, only when enlightened by this conception does man see clearly the right direction for his own activity. Man is then no longer destined to suffer and to despair, as was inevitable under the former conception.

"The universe and I in it," says a man of this conception to himself, "exist by the will of God. I cannot know the whole of the universe (for in its immensity it transcends my comprehension), nor can I know my own position in it, but I do know with certainty what God, who has sent me into the world (infinite in time and space, and therefore incomprehensible to me), demands from me. This is revealed to me (1) by the collective wisdom of the best men who have gone before me, *i.e.* by tradition, (2) by my own reason, and (3) by my heart, *i.e.* by the highest aspiration of my nature.

Tradition (the collective wisdom of my greatest forerunners) tells me that I should do unto others as I would that they should do unto me.

My reason shows me that only by all men acting thus, is the highest happiness for all men attainable.

Only when I yield myself to that intuition of love which demands obedience to this law, is my own heart happy and at rest. And not only can I then know how to act, but I can and do discern the work, to co-operate in which my activity was designed and is required.

I cannot fathom God's whole design, for the sake of which the universe exists and lives; but the divine work which is being accomplished in this world, and in which I participate by living, is comprehensible to me.

This work is the annihilation of discord and strife among men and among all creatures, and the establishment of the highest unity and concord and love.

It is the fulfilment of the promises of the Hebrew prophet who foretold a time when all men should be taught by truth, when spears should be turned into reaping hooks, swords be beaten to ploughshares, and the lion lie down with the lamb.

So that a man of Christian intelligence not only knows what he has to do, but he also understands the work he is doing.

He has to act so as to co-operate towards the establishment of the kingdom of God on earth. For this a man must obey his intuition of God's will, *i.e.* must act lovingly towards others, as he would that others should act towards him.

Thus the intuitive demands of man's soul coincide with the external aim of life, which he sees before him.

Man in this world, according to Christian teaching, is God's labourer. A labourer does not know his master's whole design, but he does know the immediate object which he is set to work at. He receives definite instructions what to do, and especially what not to do, lest he hinder the attainment of the very ends towards which his labour should tend. For the rest he has full liberty given him. And therefore for a man who has grasped the Christian conception of life, the meaning of his life is perfectly plain and reasonable, nor can he have a moment's hesitation as to *how* he should act, or *what* he should do to fulfil the object for which he lives.

And yet in spite of such a twofold indication (clear and indubitable to a man of Christian understanding) of what is the real aim and meaning of human life, and of what, men should do and should not do, we find people (and people calling themselves Christians) who decide that in such and such circumstances, men ought to abandon God's law and reason's guidance and to act in opposition to them, because (according to their conception) the effects of actions performed in submission to God's law may be detrimental or inconvenient.

According to the law, contained alike in tradition, in our reason, and in our hearts, man should always do unto others as he would that they should do unto him; he should always co-operate in the development of love and union among created beings. But, on the contrary, in the judgment of these far-sighted people, as long as it is premature in their opinion to obey this law, man should do violence, imprison or kill people, and thereby evoke anger and venom instead of loving union in the hearts of men. It is as though a bricklayer, set to do a particular task, and knowing that he was co-operating with others to build a house, after receiving clear and precise instructions from the master himself how to build a certain wall, received from some fellow-bricklayers (who like himself knew neither the plan of the house, nor what would fit in with it) orders to cease building his wall, and instead rather to pull down a wall that other workmen had erected.

Astonishing delusion! A being who breathes to-day, and has vanished to-morrow, receives one definite indubitable law to guide him through the brief term of his life; but instead of obeying that law, he prefers to fancy that he knows what is necessary, advantageous, and well timed for men, and for all the world — this world which continually moves and evolves; and for the sake of some advantage (which each man pictures after his own fancy), he decides that he and other people should, temporarily, abandon the indubitable law, given to him and to all men, and should act not as he would that others should act towards him, nor bring love into the world, but should do violence, imprison, kill, and bring into the world enmity whenever it seems to him profitable to do so.

And he decides to act thus, though he knows that the most horrible cruelties, martyrdoms, and murders—from the inquisitions, and the murders and horrors of all the revolutions, down to the brutalities of contemporary Anarchists and their slaughter by the established authorities—have only occurred because people will imagine that they know what is necessary for mankind and for the world. But are there not always, at any given moment, two opposite parties, each of which declares that it is necessary to use force against the other? The "law-and-order" party against the Anarchist, the Anarchist against the "law-and-order" men; English against Americans, and Americans against English; Germans against English, and English against Germans, and so forth in all possible combinations and rearrangements.

A man enlightened by Christianity sees that he has no reason to abandon the law of God, given to enable him to walk sure-footedly through life, in order to follow the chance, inconstant, and often contradictory demands of men. But besides this, if he has lived a Christian life for some time, and has developed in himself a moral Christian sensibility, he literally cannot act as people demand of him. Not his reason alone, but his feeling also makes it impossible.

To many people of our society, it would be impossible to torture or kill a baby, even if they were told that by so doing they could save hundreds of other people. And in the same way a man, when he has developed a Christian sensibility of heart, finds a whole series of actions become impossible for him. For instance, a Christian who is obliged to take part in judicial proceedings in which a man may be sentenced to death, or who is obliged to take part in evictions or in debating a proposal leading to war, or to participate in preparations for war (not to mention war itself), is in a position parallel to that of a kindly man called on to torture or to kill a baby. It is not reason alone that forbids him to do what is demanded of him; he feels instinctively that he *cannot* do it. For certain actions are morally impossible, just as others are physically impossible. As a man cannot lift a mountain, and as a kindly man cannot kill an infant, so a man living the

Christian life, cannot take part in deeds of violence. Of what value, then, to him are arguments about the imaginary advantages of doing what it is morally impossible for him to do?

But how is a man to act when he sees clearly the evil of following the law of love and its corollary law of Non-resistance? How (to use the stock example) is a man to act when he sees a robber killing or outraging a child, and he can only save the child by killing the robber?

When such a case is put, it is generally assumed that the only possible reply is that one should kill the robber to save the child. But this answer is given so quickly and decidedly, only because we are all so accustomed to the use of violence, not only to save a child, but even to prevent a neighbouring government altering its frontier at the expense of ours, or some one from smuggling lace across that frontier, or even to defend our garden fruit from a passer-by.

It is assumed that to save the child, the robber should be killed. But it is only necessary to consider the question, On what grounds a man (whether he be or be not a Christian) ought to act so, in order to come to the conclusion that such action has no reasonable foundation, and only seems to us necessary, because up to two thousand years ago such conduct was considered right, and a habit of acting so was formed. Why should a non-Christian, not acknowledging God, nor regarding the fulfilment of His will as the aim of life, decide to kill the robber in order to defend the child? By killing the robber he certainly kills, whereas he cannot know positively whether the robber would have killed the child or not. But letting that pass, who shall say whether the child's life was more needed, was better, than the robber's life?

Surely if the non-Christian knows not God, nor sees life's meaning in the performance of His will, the only rule for his actions must be a reckoning, a conception, of what is more profitable for him and for all men: a continuation of the robber's life or of the child's. To decide that he needs to know what would become of the child whom he saves, and what—had he not killed him—would have been the future of the robber he kills. And as he cannot know this, the non-Christian has no sufficient rational

2

ground for killing a robber to save a child.

If a man is a Christian, and consequently acknowledges God and sees the meaning of life in fulfilling His will, then, however ferocious the robber, however innocent and lovely the child, he has even less ground to abandon the God-given law and to do to the robber what the robber wishes to do to the child. He may plead with the robber, may interpose his own body between the robber and the victim, but there is one thing he cannot do: he cannot deliberately abandon the law he has received from God, the fulfilment of which alone gives meaning to his life. Very probably bad education, or his animal nature, may cause a man (Christian or non-Christian) to kill the robber, not only to save the child, but even to save himself or to save his purse, but it does not follow that he is right in acting thus, or that he should accustom himself or others to think such conduct right.

What it does show is that, notwithstanding a coating of education and of Christianity, the habits of the Stone Age are yet so strong in man, that he

still commits actions long since condemned by his reasonable conscience.

I see a robber killing a child, and I
can save the child by killing the
robber — therefore in certain cases
violence must be used to resist evil.
A man's life is in danger, and can be
saved only by my telling a lie—therefore in certain cases one must lie. A
man is starving, and one can save him
only by stealing—therefore in certain
cases one must steal.

I lately read a story by Coppée, in
which an orderly kills his officer,
whose life was insured, and thereby
saves the honour and the family of the
officer. Therefore in certain cases one
must kill.

Such inventions and the deductions
from them only prove that there are
men who know that it is not well to
steal, to lie, or to kill, but who are still
so unwilling that people should cease
to do these things, that they use all
their mental powers to invent excuses
for such conduct. There is no moral
law, concerning which we may not
devise a case in which it is difficult
to decide what is more moral: to disobey the law or to obey it? But all
such inventions fail to prove that the

laws, "thou shalt not lie, steal, or kill," are invalid.

It is the same with reference to the law of Non-resistance. People know it is wrong to use violence, but they are so anxious to continue to live a life secured by the "strong arm of the law," that—instead of devoting their intellects to the elucidation of the evils which have flowed and are still flowing from admitting that man has a right to use violence to his fellow-men —they prefer to exert their mental powers in defence of that error.

"*Fais ce que dois, advienne que pourra*" ("Do what's right, come what may") is an expression of profound wisdom. We each can know indubitably what we ought to do—but what results will follow from our actions, we none of us either do know or can know. Therefore it follows that, besides feeling the call of duty, we are further driven to act as duty bids us, by the consideration that we have no other guidance, but are totally ignorant of what will result from our actions.

Christian teaching indicates what a man should do to perform that will of Him who sent him into life; but discussion as to what results we anticipate from such or such human actions, have nothing to do with Christianity, but are just an example of the error which Christianity eliminates.

None of us has ever yet met the imaginary robber with the imaginary child, but all the horrors which fill the annals of history and of our own times came and come from this one thing—that people will believe that they can foresee the results of hypothetical future actions.

The case is this: People once lived an animal life, and violated or killed whom they thought well to violate or to kill. They even ate each other; and public opinion approved of it. Thousands of years ago, as far back as the times of Moses, a day came when people had realised that to violate or kill each other is bad. But there were people for whom the reign of force was advantageous, and these did not approve of the change, but assured themselves and others that to do deeds of violence and to kill people is not always bad, but that there are circumstances when it is necessary and even moral. And violence and even slaughter, though not so frequent or so cruel as before, continued, only with this difference, that those who committed or commended such acts, excused themselves by pleading that they did it for the benefit of humanity.

It was just this sophistical justification of violence that Christ denounced. When two enemies fight, each may think his own conduct justified by the circumstances. Excuses can be made for every use of violence; and no infallible standard has ever been discovered by which to measure the worth of these excuses. Therefore Christ taught not to believe in any excuse for violence, and (contrary to what had been taught by them of old time) never to use violence.

One would have thought that those who professed Christianity would have been indefatigable in exposing deception in this matter, for in such exposure lay one of the chief manifestations of Christianity. What really happened was just the reverse. People who profited by violence, and who did not wish to give up their advantages, took on themselves a monopoly of Christian preaching, and declared that as cases can be found in which Non-resistance causes more harm than the use of violence (the imaginary robber killing the imaginary child), therefore Christ's doctrine of Non-resistance need not always be followed, and that one may deviate from his teaching to defend one's life or the life of others; to defend one's country; to save society from lunatics or criminals; and in many other cases. The decision of the question, In what cases should Christ's teaching be set aside? was left to the very people who employed violence. So that it ended by Christ's teaching on the subject of not resisting evil by violence being completely annulled. And what was worst of all, was that the very people Christ denounced came to consider themselves the sole preachers and expositors of his doctrines. But the light shines through the darkness, and Christ's teaching is again exposing the pseudo-teachers of Christianity.

We may think about rearranging the world to suit our own taste; no one can prevent that, and we may try to do what seems to us pleasant or profitable, and with that object treat our fellow-creatures with violence, on the pretext that we are doing good. But acting thus, we cannot pretend to follow Christ's teaching, for Christ denounced just this deception. Truth sooner or later reappears, and the false teachers are shown up, which is just what is happening to-day.

Only let the question of man's life be rightly put, as Christ put it, and not as it has been perversely put by the Churches, and the whole structure of falsehood which the Churches have built over Christ's teaching will collapse of itself.

The real question is not whether it will be good or bad for a certain human society that people should follow the law of Love and the consesequent law of Non-resistance, but it is this, Do you, who to-day live and tomorrow will die (who are indeed tending deathward every moment), do you wish now, immediately and entirely, to obey the law of Him who sent you into life, and who clearly showed you His will, alike in tradition and in your mind and heart; or do you prefer to resist His will? And as soon as the question is put thus, only one reply is possible — I wish now, this moment, without delay or hesitation, to the very utmost of my strength, neither waiting for anyone, nor counting the cost, to do that which alone is clearly demanded by Him, who sent me into the world; and on no account and under no conditions do I wish to, or can I, act otherwise, for herein lies my only possibility of a rational and un-harassed life.

———

To a Private Friend.[1]

No! dear friend, you are not right; not in what you say, but in *how* you say it.

Do what you like, how you like, yet one thing only is necessary to God, to man, and to myself—it is that I should have a heart free from condemnation, contempt, irritation, irony, animosity towards men. And the devil take all this manual labour if it removes my heart from men, and does not draw me closer to them; it would be better, like a Buddhist, to go about with a bowl, begging.

But it is not for me to write this to you, for as you say when writing to

[1] The person here addressed, desiring "to get off the back of the workers" had greatly sim-plified his life, and had begun to work with his own hands; but had then fallen into the common errors, self-satisfaction, and contempt of all other reformers who did not adopt his position; and particularly of one.—*Note by Ed.*

me, so I say to you—you know all this
better than I do. And you know that
you have an ill-feeling toward our
mutual friend, and this is wrong, and
occasions you pain.

Yes, it *is* necessary that the truth
should prevail. This is most important, and God knows it, and has put us
into such conditions that we cannot
escape from the truth; we cannot
escape physical and yet less moral
sufferings, neither can we escape death.
And we are all *in* this truth, and our
friend also, and one cannot say about
anyone that he is in falsehood. To
say that he is in falsehood is the same
as to say that he is in the mire, and to
therefore abandon him. If he be in
the mire, then so much the more should
we pity and cleanse him; he cannot
like it any more than any of us.

You say that "where two or three
are gathered in My name," there alone
is life. Not so. Life is also in him
who for twenty-five years has been
sitting alone in prison, and on a tower.

But this is neither here nor there;
what I want to say above all is this—

The *living* man is he who continues
advancing in the direction illuminated
by the lantern which advances in front

of him, and who never attains the limit of the illuminated space continually receding before him. This is life, and there is no other. And only in this life is there no death, because the lantern illuminates the hereafter, and one follows it there with the same peace one does during the whole of life. But if a man veils the lamp, and directs its rays to the space immediately around or behind him, but not in front of him, and ceases to advance, then there will be cessation of life.

Pardon me, my friend, and accept this with the same love with which I am writing it : I am afraid that having attained that which your lamp has for so long been showing, you have ceased to carry it in front of you. God forbid. Why, this is the eternal deception. As we continually wish to achieve something external, to accomplish some definite purpose, so also do we continue to wish to attain the best position and to establish ourselves .in it; but as it is impossible as well as unnecessary to accomplish any definite purpose, but only necessary to adapt one's powers in the best way to God's eternal work— so also can there be no position either better or worse, but every position is only a certain result at a certain time, of my relation to God's work, and there cannot be any one permanent position; your present position is neither more nor less justifiable than the one you were in when you lived in T——, and it will certainly be replaced by another one.

Take care, old fellow! Do not get angry with me, and do not fire a charge at me as you did at our friend, but on the contrary reconcile yourself to him.

———

A Further Letter to the same Friend.

I wrote to you in a bad weak state of mind, and therefore both what I wrote was not clear and I did not come to the chief point I was driving at. The point was this—

In order to live it is absolutely necessary to advance in a work in which there is no end, and in the accomplishment of which there are no obstacles. And there is only one such work: perfection in love. Manual labour in certain conditions is only *in some cases* the result of love. Such labour and restricted economical conditions are the results, and therefore the verification, of true life; the absence of labour and an elevated assured economical position demonstrate the insincerity and untruthfulness and weakness of the man. The contrary of this has, therefore, a negative significance, but no positive significance.

The idolatry of labour is a dangerous error and a most habitual one.

Prayer, as the result of one's aspiration towards God, is a most lawful act; but when it becomes an aim in itself, it produces ritual, which kills the moral life.

Mercy, help afforded one's neighbour as the result of love to God, is a most lawful thing; but when it becomes an aim in itself, it produces philanthropy.

Want, poverty, absence of property, as the result of abstinence from violent resistance and of renunciation of independent means, is a most lawful state; but when it is placed as a necessary condition, as an aim in itself, it produces the formal poverty of Buddhists and of monks.

It is the same with manual labour. Such labour as the result of the renunciation of independent means and of the desire to serve others, is a lawful thing, but if it becomes an aim in itself, it will inevitably lead to evil.[1]

But, above all—above all, I say to you from soul to soul, dear friend, the chief aim, infinite, joyful, always attainable, and worthy of the powers which are given us, is the increase of love.

And increase of love is attainable by one definite effort; by the cleansing of one's soul from all that is personal, lustful, inimical. "The human soul is Christian," it has been said; *i.e.* love is not only natural to it, but its very essence is love; and therefore in order to strengthen, augment love, it is only necessary to cleanse the soul, to polish it, like a glass for collecting rays. The more polished and clean it is, the more powerfully will it transmit and focus the light and warmth of love.

And this work has no end, no obstacles, its joy is unlimited, and there is nothing good, nothing that a man *should* do which does not enter as a part into this work,—the work of cleansing one's soul and thus increasing love.

You know this, dear friend, you know this joy, for you have been

[1] See also Tolstoy's letter on "Communal Life" in *Some Social Remedies*, uniform with this. —*Note by Ed.*

advancing along this way, and are at present probably advancing, in the depth of your consciousness. I, for my part, the nearer I approach to bodily death the clearer I see this and recognise it, not only in contemplation but in actual experience. I am learning— not only towards living men who are present, but towards those absent, and towards animals, towards dead people —to repress in myself every shade of contempt, irony, irritation, not to speak of animosity; and it is wonderful how in the measure of one's attainment of this one is recompensed by lucidity of thought, by joy of life, by fruitfulness, adaptiveness of labour.

In this work, you probably know this —ill-feeling towards one man paralyses the powers of life in the same way as ill-feeling, hatred, towards the whole human race. The glass is dimmed, and does not transmit light owing to one piece of dirt as well as to a whole barrowful.

———

ON COMPROMISE.

It is always said, when a man has not attained that after which he has been striving, when he has not drawn

a straight line, precisely the shortest
between two points, or even when he
has drawn quite a crooked and broken
line, instead of a straight one, thus:
〰️ —, it is said that he is com-
promising.

Even the man himself often regards
it as a compromise, and is grieved by
it. But a great confusion is taking
place here, and in connection with the
most important conceptions.

A sincere, truly - living man can
never walk otherwise than thus:
〰️ (may he only not walk

thus : 〰️). Deviation from
the law (the ideal) in its application in
practice is not criminal, but inevitable,
and is not a compromise in the sense
of something wrong. A compromise is
the acknowledgment beforehand that
one is at present unable to fulfil the
whole law—an entirely straight line;
and only such a compromise is wrong.
To admit beforehand, for instance, that
violence, property, religious worship,
divorce, etc., are sometimes necessary,
then only is it that this happens:
〰️ , *i.e.* there appears a double
confusion in the life.

Let us suppose that I know and believe that I may never and nowhere possess any kind of property, and so also with regard to violence, the desertion of my wife, bodily impurity, etc., and I live on and on, and, judging by my past experience and my observation of others, I foresee that I·shall not prevail in all, but shall sin; yet I hope, pray God, and am determined to go straight; I wish to go straight, but I *sin*; this appears as sin, I know it as such, and repent of it, but I am guilty of no compromise, no *deception* before God.

Deception would be much worse than sin, it would be blasphemy against the Holy Ghost. And the reason is evident. From the former I shall suffer alone, and my suffering will be to my profit, will, hour by hour, day by day (and one probably experiences this on looking back), draw me nearer to God; whereas from the latter others will suffer, and both they and I shall depart farther and farther from Him.

I repeat, in practice the theory or ideal is never perfectly fulfilled; in other words, that man never attains perfection, but only approaches towards it. It is impossible to draw a mathematically straight line,—all lines are

3

but approximations to the ideal; such
incomplete fulfilment of the ideal is
the inevitable condition of life, and is
not sin, — everyone advances towards
the ideal according to his powers.

But concession, or compromise in
theory, is a great sin. If I, knowing
that a straight line is a mathematical
conception, try to draw one, I shall
attain an approximation to a straight
line; but if, seeing that it is impossible
to draw a perfectly straight line, I
decide that I may deviate from the
ideal of the straight line, then I stray
away, God knows where. It is the
same with moral principles.

If, in principle, I refuse to admit my
right to commit violence against men,
in any case, then I approach abstinence
from violence; but if I admit that one
may use violence towards a madman
(it is difficult to define madness, and to
say when one may and when one may
not resort to violence), then I risk
deviating very far from the law of
Non-resistance.

So with property. If I admit—as
it is repeatedly stated in the Gospels,
and as it is evident from the whole of
Christ's teaching—that I may not hold
property, then, even although I wear

clothing which I regard as my own, as long as no one asserts his right to it, and so on, I shall be near to the law of Christ; but as soon as I admit in principle the right of property, I may very easily, in defending it, depart yet farther from the law of Non-resistance.

An example of such a deviation, or compromise, may be found in Matt. v. 22, where the words "without a cause" have been added.

No living man will ever fulfil the will of God perfectly. But because we see and know the impossibility of completely fulfilling God's will, it does not follow that we should determine beforehand to fulfil it incompletely, partially (this is a most common and dreadful sin). But we should, on the contrary, incessantly and always strive for its complete fulfilment. "Seek ye first the kingdom of God and His righteousness, and all things needful will be added unto you."

The question of utility must be altogether set aside by the Christian. No one can decide questions of utility, —who will be benefited, and in what way. Utility is beyond our power; but what we should do for the accomplishment of the Father's will,—this we know, and this we must do.

What you say about your activity—about the necessity, or rather advantage of making certain compromises, simply in order that you may be able to continue your activity, does not convince me.

The most precious thing you possess, and that you are able to possess, is your soul, your spiritual personality, and this is also the most powerful instrument of your influence over others; therefore the lowering of your spiritual personality (and every conscious compromise is such a lowering) cannot, for any purpose, be advantageous.

I am so alarmed at those customary, pernicious compromises, which deprive life of all its significance, that I challenge this foe everywhere, and attack him, especially when I hear considerations as to the apparent utility we attain. It always seems to me that as the definite purpose of the life of mankind is not revealed to us, neither is the true result of our actions revealed to us; but what is revealed is that which we must do for the satisfaction of the inner demands of our conscience. "*Fais ce que dois, advienne que pourra*" ("Do what you ought, happen what may").

The Figure Repeated.

For man to do that which he regards as evil is not only natural, but inevitable, because, as man's life advances, —as he grows morally,—he discovers that to be evil which he used formerly to do, and he retains the habit of that evil. Man wishes to draw a straight line, but his hand trembles, and the line becomes crooked. But if a man were to say to himself, "Well, I cannot succeed with a straight line, so I will not attempt it, but will just draw where my hand leads me,"—then the result would be very dreadful.

Deviation from that which one wishes to accomplish is the inevitable condition of every activity; but the false argument as to the evil which I commit,— in the depth of my soul knowing it to be evil,—that it is good, this is very, very dangerous.

In practical life one cannot avoid inexactness, departure from the ideal; but in one's consciousness, in the ideal itself, if there be any departures it is disastrous; if, in one's imagination, at least, a straight line be not the shortest distance between two points.

———

From the Private MS. Diary.

There is only one way of serving mankind. That is, to become better yourself. "Let your light so shine before men, that they may see your good works, and glorify your Father which is in heaven." A man cannot denounce sin while standing in the mire of sin.

. . . . .

The problem for us all is one and the same: From our position of property, with our many wants, and absence of work useful to mankind,— to learn to live with fewer demands, without the wish for more, and to learn to do work that is unquestionably useful to men. And to this we must descend by degrees, that is, according to our attainment in the one direction and the other.

. . . . .

To be useful to men! How? Not with money; not even by doing material services. To sweep a skating rink, make boots, wash clothes, sit for

a night with a sick person? Perhaps.
All these acts may be good, and are
better done for others than for oneself;
but they may be bad, and, strictly
speaking, are not absolutely necessary.
One thing is undoubtedly useful and
necessary, namely, to teach men to
live rightly. But how to do that?
There is one way—to live rightly
oneself. Our error is, that men wish
to teach so that the teaching shall
be seen in visible results; to which
end one must inevitably teach by
words. But to teach by one's life is
the surest of sure ways; only often,
almost always, one will not see the
fruit. One thing remains then: to
live rightly. Help me, God!

People are for ever finding they
cannot live together.

"I cannot live with him." "Ah,
you cannot? Then give up living
altogether, for it is precisely with him
you are meant to live." Or, "I wish
to plough,—only not this field" (which
is the first that has to be ploughed).
"Then it seems you are only pretending, and that you do not wish to
plough."

So it was with me, in regard to

many and many people. "I cannot live with him; I will leave him, that will be better." But how can it be better, when it is the worst thing that could possibly be done?

Everything, poor living, self-denial, hard work, humility itself,—everything is necessary for no other end than to enable one to live with mankind; to live with them, that is, to love them. But if there be no love, then all the rest is worthless. All our ploughing is done so that what is sown may spring up; but if we trample the young crops, then where was the good of ploughing?

PRINTED BY
MORRISON AND GIBB LIMITED, EDINBURGH

THREEPENCE

Patriotism .
and . . .
Government

By Leo
Colstoy

The Free Age Press
1900

The Free Age Press stands for an attempt to assist in spreading those deep convictions in which the noblest spirits of every age and race have united—that man's true aim and happiness is "unity in reason and love"; the realisation of the brotherhood of all men—and that we *must* all strive to purge away, each from himself, those false ideas, false feelings, and false desires, personal, social, religious, political, racial, economic, which alienate us one from another and produce nine-tenths of the sum of human suffering.

Of these truly Christian and universally religious aspirations the writings of Leo Tolstoy are perhaps to-day the most definite expression, and it is to the production of 1d., 3d., and 6d. editions of all his known religious, social, and ethical works, together with the unpublished matter and future writings to which we have and shall have special access (being in close relationship with Tolstoy), that *The Free Age Press* will at first devote itself; trusting that all who sympathise will assist by every means in their power, especially in helping to spread the books the world over, losing no opportunity of introducing them whenever and wherever feasible, and of so making it possible for the work to be continued, and extended into wider and wider fields. As it is Tolstoy's desire that his books shall not be copyrighted, our editions will, whenever possible, be free to the world.

Suggestions, criticisms, inquiries, offers of help and co-operation will be gratefully welcomed; and it is specially requested that the names of any books that have helped towards a better understanding of life may be furnished, so that a much needed list may be compiled and published.

Letters, Private Orders, and Money Orders (it is hoped that friends will *purchase* as many copies as possible : even one will help) should be addressed to THE EDITORS, "FREE AGE PRESS," MALDON, ESSEX. *Booksellers* must order from Messrs. SIMPKIN, MARSHALL, HAMILTON, KENT, & Co. LTD., London, E.C. ; THE CLARION CO. LTD., 72 Fleet Street, E.C. ; Messrs. JOHN MENZIES & Co., Glasgow ; and Mr. JOHN HEYWOOD, Manchester.

PATRIOTISM
AND GOVERNMENT

PATRIOTISM .

AND . . . .

GOVERNMENT

By LEO . .

TOLSTOY .

Translated by . .

AYLMER MAUDE

THE FREE AGE PRESS

MALDON, ESSEX . . . .

1900

" *The time was fast approaching when to call a man a patriot woula be the deepest insult you could offer him. Patriotism now meant aa-vocating plunder in the interests of the privileged classes of the particular State system into which we had happened to be born.*"

E. Belfort Bax.

PATRIOTISM AND
GOVERNMENT

—•—

CHAPTER I

I HAVE already several times expressed the
thought that the feeling of patriotism is in
our day an unnatural, irrational, and harmful feeling, and is the cause of a great part
of the ills from which mankind is suffering; and that, consequently, this feeling
should not be cultivated, as is now being
done, but should, on the contrary, be suppressed and eradicated by all means avail-
able to rational men.   Yet, strange to say,
though it is undeniable that the universal
armaments and the destructive wars which
are ruining the peoples result from that
one feeling, all my arguments showing
the backwardness, anachronism, and harmfulness of patriotism have been met, and
are still met, either by silence, or by in-
tentional misconception, or by a strange
unvarying reply to the effect that only bad

5

patriotism (Jingoism, or Chauvinism) is bad, but that real, good patriotism is a very elevated moral feeling, to condemn which is not only irrational but wicked.

As to what this real, good patriotism consists of nothing at all is said; or, if anything is said, instead of explanation we get declamatory, inflated phrases; or, finally, something else is substituted for patriotism, something which has nothing in common with the patriotism we all know, and from the results of which we all suffer so severely.

It is generally said that the real, good patriotism consists in desiring for one's own people or State such real benefits as do not infringe the well-being of other nations.

Talking, recently, to an Englishman about the present war, I said to him that the real cause of the war was not avarice, as is generally said, but patriotism, as is evident from the temper of the whole English society. The Englishman did not agree with me, and said that even were the case so, it resulted from the fact that the patriotism at present inspiring Englishmen is a bad patriotism; but that good patriotism, such as he was imbued with, consists in Englishmen, his compatriots, acting well.

"Then do you wish only Englishmen to act well?" I asked.

"I wish all men to do so," said he; indicating clearly by that reply the characteristic of true benefits,—whether moral, scientific, or even material and practical,—which is that they spread out to all men; and therefore to wish such benefits to anyone, not only is not patriotic, but is the reverse of patriotic.

Neither are the peculiarities of each people patriotism; though these things are purposely substituted for the conception of patriotism by its defenders. They say that the peculiarities of each people are an essential condition of human progress, and that therefore patriotism, which seeks to maintain those peculiarities is a good and useful feeling. But is it not quite evident that if, once upon a time, these peculiarities of each people—these customs, creeds, languages—were conditions necessary for the life of humanity,·yet in our time these same peculiarities form the chief obstacle to what is already recognised as an ideal—the brotherly union of the peoples? And therefore the maintenance and defence of any nationality—Russian, German, French, or Anglo-Saxon, provoking the corresponding maintenance and defence not only of Hungarian, Polish, and Irish nationalities, but also of Basque, Provençal, Mordvinian, Tchouvásh, and many other nationalities—serves not to harmonise and unite men, but to estrange and divide them more and more from one another.

So that not the imaginary but the real patriotism, which we all know, by which most people to-day are swayed, and from which humanity suffers so severely, is not the wish for spiritual benefits for one's own people (it is impossible to desire spiritual benefits for one's own people only); but it is a very definite feeling of preference for one's own people or State above all other peoples and States, and therefore it is the wish to get for that people or State the greatest advantages and power that can be got; and these are always obtainable only at the expense of the advantages and power of other peoples or States.

It would therefore seem obvious that patriotism as a feeling, is a bad and harmful feeling, and as a doctrine is a stupid doctrine. For it is clear that if each people and each State considers itself the best of peoples and States, they all dwell in a gross and harmful delusion.

———

CHAPTER II

ONE would expect the harmfulness and irrationality of patriotism to be evident to people. But the surprising fact is that cultured and learned men not only do not notice it for themselves, but they contest every exposure of the harm and stupidity of patriotism with the greatest obstinacy and ardour, though without any rational grounds; and they continue to belaud it as beneficent and elevating.

What does this mean?

Only one explanation of this amazing fact presents itself to me.

All human history from the earliest times and to our day may be considered as a movement of the consciousness, both of individuals and of homogeneous groups, from lower ideas to higher ones.

The whole path, travelled both by individuals and by homogeneous groups, may be represented as a consecutive flight of steps from the very lowest, on the level of animal life, to the very highest to which the consciousness of man has attained at a given moment of history.

Each man, like each separate homogeneous group, nation, or State, always moved and moves up this ladder of ideas. Some portions of humanity move on, others lag far behind, others, again,—the majority,—move somewhere between the most advanced and the most backward. But all, on whatever step they stand, are inevitably and irresistibly moving from lower to higher ideas. And always, at any given moment, both the individuals and the separate groups of people — advanced, middle, or backward—stand in three different relations to three stages of ideas, amid which they move.

Always, both for the individual and for the separate groups of people, there are the ideas of the past, which are worn out and have become strange to them, and to which they cannot revert: as, for instance, in our Christian world the ideas of cannibalism, universal plunder, the rape of

wives, and other customs of which only
a record remains.

And there are the ideas of the present,
instilled into men's minds by education,
by example, and by the general activity of
all around them: ideas under the power
of which they live at a given time; for
instance, in our own day, the ideas of
property, State organisation, trade, utilisa-
tion of domestic animals, etc.

And there are the ideas of the future,
of which some are already approaching
realisation, and are obliging people to
change their way of life and to struggle
against the former ways: such ideas in
our world as those of freeing the labourers,
of giving equality to women, and of dis-
using flesh food, etc.; while others, though
already recognised, have not yet begun to
struggle against the old forms of life: such
in our time are the ideas (which we call
ideals) of the extermination of violence,
the arrangement of a communal system of
property, of a universal religion, and of
a general brotherhood of men.

And, therefore, every man and every
homogeneous group of men, on whatever
level they may stand, having behind them
the worn-out remembrances of the past, and
before them the ideals of the future, are
always in a state of struggle between the
moribund ideas of the present and the
ideas of the future that are coming to life.
It usually happens that when an idea
which has been useful and even necessary
in the past becomes superfluous, that idea

after a more or less prolonged struggle yields its place to a new idea which was till then an ideal, but which thus becomes a present idea.

But it does occur that an antiquated idea, already replaced in people's consciousness by a higher one, is of such a kind that its maintenance is profitable to certain people who have the greatest influence in their society. And then it happens that this antiquated idea, though it is in sharp contradiction to the whole surrounding form of life which has been altering in other respects, continues to influence people and to sway their actions. Such retention of antiquated ideas always occurred and still occurs in the region of religion. The cause is that the priests, whose profitable positions are bound up with the antiquated religious idea, using their power, purposely hold people to the antiquated idea.

The same thing occurs, and for similar reasons, in the political sphere, with reference to the patriotic idea, on which every dominion is based. People to whom it is profitable to do so, maintain that idea by artificial means, though it now lacks both sense and utility. And as these people possess the most powerful means of influencing others, they are able to achieve their object.

In this, it seems to me, lies the explanation of the strange contrast between the antiquated patriotic idea, and the whole drift of ideas making in a contrary direction which have already entered into the consciousness of the Christian world.

———

Chapter III

Patriotism as a feeling of exclusive love for one's own people, and as a doctrine of the virtue of sacrificing one's tranquillity, one's property, and even one's life, in defence of the weak among them from slaughter and outrage by their enemies, was the highest idea of the period when each nation considered it feasible and just, to subject to slaughter and outrage the people of other nations for its own advantage.

But already, some two thousand years ago, humanity, in the person of the highest representatives of its wisdom, began to recognise the higher idea of a brotherhood of man; and that idea penetrating man's consciousness more and more, has in our time attained most varied forms of realisation. Thanks to improved means of communication, and to the unity of industry, of trade, of the arts, and of science, —men to-day are so bound one to another that the danger of conquest, massacre, or outrage by a neighbouring people has quite disappeared, and all peoples (the peoples, but not the governments) live together in peaceful, mutually advantageous, friendly, commercial, industrial, artistic, and scientific relations, which they

have no need and no desire to disturb.
And, therefore, one would think that the
antiquated feeling of patriotism—being
superfluous and incompatible with the
consciousness we have reached of the
existence of brotherhood among men of
different nationalities — should dwindle
more and more until it completely disappears. Yet the very opposite of this
occurs : this harmful and antiquated feeling not only continues to exist, but burns
more and more fiercely.

The peoples, without any reasonable
ground, and contrary alike to their conception of right and to their own advantage, not only sympathise with governments in their attacks on other nations, in
their seizures of foreign possessions, and
in defending by force what they have
already stolen, but even themselves demand
such attacks, seizures, and defences ; are
glad of them ; and take pride in them.
The small oppressed nationalities which
have fallen under the power of the great
States, — the Poles, Irish, Bohemians,
Fins, or Armenians,—reacting against the
patriotism of their conquerors, which is the
cause of their oppression, catch from their
oppressors the infection of this feeling of
patriotism,—which has ceased to be necessary, and is now obsolete, unmeaning, and
harmful,—and catch it to such a degree that
all their activity is concentrated upon it, and
they, themselves suffering from the patriotism of the stronger nations, are ready to
perpetrate on other peoples, for the sake of

this same patriotism, the very same deeds
that their oppressors have perpetrated and
are perpetrating on them.

This occurs because the ruling classes
(including not only the actual rulers with
their officials, but all the classes who
enjoy an exceptionally advantageous position—the capitalists, journalists, and most
of the artists and scientists) can retain
their position,—exceptionally advantageous
in comparison with that of the labouring
masses,—thanks only to the government
organisation, which rests on patriotism.
They have in their hands all the most
powerful means of influencing the people,
and always sedulously support patriotic
feelings in themselves and in others, more
especially as those feelings which uphold
the government's power, are those that are
always best rewarded by that power.

Every official prospers in his career the
better the more patriotic he is; so also
the army man gets promotion in time of
war; and war is produced by patriotism.

Patriotism and its result—wars, give an
enormous revenue to the newspaper trade,
and profits to many other trades. Every
writer, teacher, and professor is more
secure in his place the more he preaches
patriotism. Every emperor and king obtains the more fame the more he is addicted
to patriotism.

The ruling classes have in their hands
the army, money, the schools, the churches,
and the press. In the schools they kindle
patriotism in the children by means of

histories describing their own people as the best of all peoples, and always in the right. Among adults they kindle it by spectacles, jubilees, monuments, and by a lying patriotic press. Above all, they inflame patriotism in this way : perpetrating every kind of injustice and harshness against other nations, they provoke in them enmity towards their own people, and then in turn exploit that enmity to embitter their own people against the foreigner.

The intensification of that terrible feeling of patriotism has gone on among the European peoples in a rapidly increasing progression, and in our time has reached the utmost limits, beyond which there is nowhere for it to extend.

CHAPTER IV

WITHIN the memory of people not yet old, an occurrence took place showing most obviously the amazing intoxication caused by patriotism among the people of Christendom.

The ruling classes of Germany excited the patriotism of the masses of their people to such a degree that, in the second half of the nineteenth century, a law was proposed in accordance with which all the men had to become soldiers ; all the sons, husbands, fathers, learned men, and godly men, had to learn to murder ; to become submissive

slaves of the first man of superior military
rank they met, and be absolutely ready to
kill whomsoever they were ordered to kill; ·
to kill men of oppressed nationalities, and
their own working men standing up for
their rights, and even their own fathers
and brothers,—as was publicly proclaimed
by that most barefaced of potentates,
William II.

That horrible measure, outraging all .
man's best feelings in the grossest manner,
was, under the influence of patriotism,
acquiesced in without murmur by the
people of Germany. It resulted in their
victory over the French. That victory
yet further excited the patriotism of
Germany, and afterwards of France, Russia,
and the other Powers; and all the men
of the continental countries unresistingly
submitted to the introduction of general
military service, *i.e.* to a state of slavery,
involving a degree of humiliation and
submission incomparably worse than any
slavery of the ancient world. After this
servile submission of the masses to the
calls of patriotism, the audacity, cruelty,
and insanity of the governments knew no
bounds. A competition in the usurpation
of other people's lands in Asia, Africa, and
America began,—evoked partly by whim,
partly by vanity, and partly by covetous-
ness,—and was accompanied by ever greater
and greater distrust and enmity between
the governments.

The destruction of the people on the
lands seized, was accepted as a quite natural

proceeding. The only question was who should be first in seizing other people's land and destroying the inhabitants. All the governments not only most evidently infringed, and are infringing, the elementary demands of justice in relation to the conquered peoples, and in relation to one another, but they were guilty and continue to be guilty, of every kind of cheating, swindling, bribing, fraud, spying, robbery, and murder; and the peoples not only sympathised, and still sympathise, with them in all this, but they rejoice when it is their own government and not another government that commits such crimes.

The mutual enmity between the different peoples and States has reached, latterly, such amazing dimensions, that, notwithstanding the fact that there is no reason why one State should attack another, everyone knows that all the governments stand with their claws out and showing their teeth, and only waiting for someone to fall into trouble, or become weak, in order to tear him to pieces with as little risk as possible.

All the peoples of the so-called Christian world have been reduced by patriotism to such a state of brutality, that not only those who are obliged to kill or be killed desire slaughter and rejoice in murder, but all the people of Europe and America, living peaceably in their homes exposed to no danger, are, at each war—thanks to easy means of communication, and to the press—in the position of the spectators in a Roman circus, and, like them, delight in the slaughter, and raise the blooodthirsty cry, "*Pollice verso.*"[1]

Not adults only, but also children, pure, wise children, rejoice, according to their nationality, when they hear that the number killed and lacerated by lyddite or other shells is not seven hundred but one thousand Englishmen or Boers.

And parents (I know of such cases) encourage their children in such brutality.

But that is not all. Every increase in the army of one nation (and every nation being in danger seeks to increase its army for patriotic reasons) obliges its neighbours to increase their army, also from patriotism, and this evokes a fresh increase by the first nation.

And the same thing occurs with fortifications and navies; one State has built ten ironclads, a neighbour builds eleven; then the first builds twelve, and so on to infinity.

"I'll pinch you." "And I'll punch your head." "And I'll stab you with a dagger." "And I'll bludgeon you." "And I'll shoot you," . . . only bad children, drunken men, or animals quarrel or fight so, but yet it is just what is going on among the highest representatives of the most enlightened governments, the very men who undertake to direct the education and the morality of their subjects.

---

[1] *Pollice verso* ("thumb down") was the sign given in the Roman amphitheatres by the spectators who wished a defeated gladiator to be slain.—*Trans.*

Chapter V

THE position is becoming worse and worse, and there is no stopping this descent towards evident perdition.

The one way of escape believed in by credulous people has now been closed by recent events. I refer to the Hague Conference and to the war between England and the Transvaal which immediately followed it.

If people who think little, or but superficially, were able to comfort themselves with the idea that international courts of arbitration would supersede wars and ever-increasing armaments, the Hague Conference and the war that followed it demonstrated in the most obvious manner the impossibility of finding a solution of the difficulty in that way. After the Hague Conference it became obvious that as long as governments with armies exist, the termination of armaments and of wars is impossible. That an agreement should become possible, it is necessary that the parties to it should trust each other. And in order that the Powers should trust each other, they must lay down their arms, as the *parlementaires* do when they meet for a conference.

So long as governments, distrusting one another, not only do not disband or decrease their armies, but always increase them in correspondence with augmentations made by their neighbours, and by

means of spies watch every movement
of troops, knowing that each of the
Powers will attack its neighbour as soon
as it sees its way to do so,—no agreement is possible, and every conference is
either a stupidity, or a pastime, or a
fraud, or an impertinence, or all these
together.

It was particularly becoming for the
Russian rather than any other government to be the *enfant terrible* of the
Hague Conference. No one at home
being allowed to reply to all its evidently
mendacious manifestations and rescripts,
the Russian Government is so spoilt, that
having without the least scruple ruined
its own people with armaments, strangled
Poland, plundered Turkestan and China,
and while specially engaged in suffocating
Finland, it proposed disarmament to the
governments, in full assurance that it
would be trusted.

But strange, unexpected, and indecent
as such a proposal was, especially at the
very time when orders were being given
to increase its army, the words publicly
uttered in the hearing of the people were
such, that for the sake of appearances the
governments of the other Powers could
not decline the comical and evidently
insincere consultation, and the delegates
met, knowing in advance that nothing
would come of it, and for several weeks,
during which they drew good salaries,
though they were laughing in their
sleeves, they all conscientiously pretended

to be much occupied in arranging peace among the nations.

The Hague Conference ending as it did in the terrible bloodshed of the Transvaal War, which no one attempted, or is now attempting, to stop, was, nevertheless, of some use, though not at all in the way expected of it; it was useful because it showed in the most obvious manner that the evils from which the peoples are suffering cannot be cured by governments. That governments, even if they wished to, can terminate neither armaments nor wars.

Governments to have a reason for existing must defend their people from other people's attack; but not one people wishes to attack, or does attack, another. And, therefore, governments, far from wishing for peace, carefully excite the anger of other nations against themselves. And having excited other people's anger against themselves, and stirred up the patriotism of their own people, each government then assures its people that it is in danger, and must be defended.

And having the power in their hands, the governments can both irritate other nations and excite patriotism at home, and they carefully do both the one and the other; nor can they act otherwise, for their existence depends on thus acting.

If, in former times, governments were necessary to defend their people from other people's attacks, now, on the contrary, the governments artificially disturb the peace that exists among the peoples, and provoke enmity among them.

When it was necessary to plough in order to sow, ploughing was wise; but evidently it is absurd and harmful to go on ploughing after the seed has been sown. But this is just what the governments are obliging their people to do: to infringe the unity which exists, and which nothing would infringe if there were no governments.

———

Chapter VI

In reality what are these governments, without which people think they could not exist?

There may have been a time when such governments were necessary, and when the evil of supporting a government was less than that of being defenceless against organised neighbours; but now such governments have become unnecessary, and are a far greater evil than all the dangers with which they frighten their subjects.

Not only military governments, but governments in general, could be, I will not say useful, but at least harmless, only if they consisted of immaculate, holy people; as is theoretically the case among the Chinese. But then governments, by the nature of their activity, which consists in committing acts of violence,[1] are always composed of elements the most contrary to holiness;—of the most audacious, unscrupulous, and perverted people.

A government, therefore, and specially a government entrusted with military power, is the most dangerous organisation possible.

The government in the widest sense, including capitalists and press, is nothing else than an organisation which places the greatest part of the people in the power of a smaller part who dominate them; that smaller part is subject to a yet smaller part, and that again to a yet smaller, and so on, reaching at last a few people, or one single man, who by means of military force has power over all the rest. So that all this organisation resembles a cone, of which all the parts are completely in the power of those people, or of that one person, who are, or is, at the apex.

The apex of the cone is seized by those people, or by that person, who are, or who is, more cunning, audacious, and unscrupulous than the rest, or by someone who happens to be the heir of those who were audacious and unscrupulous.

---

[1] The word *government* in English is frequently used in an indefinite sense as almost equivalent to management or direction; but in the sense in which the word is used in the present article, the characteristic feature of government is that it claims a moral right to inflict physical penalties, and by its decree to make murder a good action.—*Trans.*

To-day it may be Borís Godunóf,[1] and
to-morrow Gregory Otrépief.[2] To-day the
licentious Catherine, who, with her para-
mours, has murdered her husband; to-
morrow Pougatchéf;[3] then Paul the madman, Nicholas I., and Alexander III.

To-day it may be Napoleon, to-morrow
a Bourbon or an Orleans, a Boulanger, or a
Panama Company; to-day it may be Glad-
stone, to-morrow Salisbury, Chamberlain,
or Rhodes.

And to such governments is allowed
full power, not only over property and
lives, but even over the spiritual and
moral development, the education, and the
religious guidance of everybody.

People construct such a terrible machine
of power, they allow anyone who can, to
seize it (and the chances always are that it
will be seized by the most morally worthless)—they slavishly submit to him, and
are then surprised that evil comes of it.
They are afraid of Anarchists' bombs, and
are not afraid of this terrible organisation
which is always threatening them with
the greatest calamities.

People found it useful to tie themselves
together in order to resist their enemies, as

---

[1] Borís Godunóf, brother-in-law of the weak Tsar
Feódor, succeeded in becoming Tsar, and reigned in
Moscow from 1598 to 1605.—*Trans.*

[2] Gregory Otrépief was a pretender who, pass-
ing himself off as Dimítry, son of Iván the
Terrible, reigned in Moscow in 1605 and 1606.—
Trans.

[3] Pougatchéf, the leader of a most formidable
insurrection, was executed in Moscow in 1775.—
Trans.

the Circassians[1] did when resisting attacks. But the danger is quite past, and yet people go on tying themselves together.

They carefully tie themselves so that one man can have them at his mercy; then they throw away the end of the rope that ties them and leave it trailing, for some rascal or fool to seize and to do them whatever harm he likes.

Really, what are people doing but just that, when they set up, submit to, and maintain an organised and military government ?

CHAPTER VII

To deliver men from the terrible evils of armaments and wars, which are always increasing and increasing, what is wanted are neither congresses nor conferences, nor treaties, nor courts of arbitration, but the destruction of those instruments of violence which are called governments, and from which humanity's greatest evils result.

To destroy governmental *violence* only one thing is needed : it is that people should understand that the feeling of

[1] The Circassians, when surrounded, used to tie themselves together leg to leg, that none might escape, but all die fighting. Instances of this kind occurred when their country was being annexed by Russia.—*Trans.*

patriotism, which alone supports that
instrument of violence, is a rude, harmful,
disgraceful, and bad feeling, and above all
—is immoral.   It is a rude feeling,
because it is one natural only to people
standing on the lowest level of morality,
and expecting from other nations those
outrages which they themselves are ready
to inflict on others; it is a harmful feeling,
because it disturbs advantageous and
joyous peaceful relations with other
peoples, and above all it produces that
governmental organisation under which
power may fall, and does fall, into the
hands of the worst men; it is a disgraceful feeling, because it turns man not
merely into a slave, but into a fighting
cock, a bull, or a gladiator, who wastes his
strength and his life for objects which are
not his own but his governments'; and it
is an immoral feeling, because, instead of
confessing oneself a son of God, as Christianity teaches us, or even a free man
guided by his own reason, each man
under the influence of patriotism confesses
himself the son of his fatherland and the
slave of his government, and commits
actions contrary to his reason and his
conscience.

It is only necessary that people should
understand this, and the terrible bond,
called government, by which we are
chained together, will fall to pieces of
itself, without struggle; and with it will
cease the terrible and useless evils it
produces.

And people are already beginning to
understand this. This, for instance, is
what a citizen of the United States
writes :—

"We are farmers, mechanics, merchants,
manufacturers, teachers, and all we ask is
the privilege of attending to our own
business. We own our homes, love our
friends, are devoted to our families, and do
not interfere with our neighbours—we have
work to do, and wish to work.

"Leave us alone!

"But they will not—these politicians.
They insist on governing us and living off
our labour. They tax us, eat our substance, conscript us, draft our boys into
their wars. All the myriads of men who
live off the government, depend upon the
government to tax us, and in order to tax
us successfully, standing armies are maintained. The plea that the army is needed
for the protection of the country is pure
fraud and pretence. The French Government affrights the people by telling them
that the Germans are ready and anxious to
fall upon them; the Russians fear the
British; the British fear everybody; and
now in America, we are told we must
increase our navy and add to our army
because Europe may at any moment com-
bine against us.

"This is fraud and untruth. The plain
people in France, Germany, England, and
America are opposed to war. We only
wish to be let alone. Men with wives,
children, sweethearts, homes, aged parents,

do not want to go off and fight some one. We are peaceable and we fear war; we hate it.

"We would like to obey the Golden Rule.

"War is the sure result of the existence of armed men. That country which maintains a large standing army will sooner or later have a war on hand. The man who prides himself on fisticuffs is going some day to meet a man who considers himself the better man, and they will fight. Germany and France have no issue save a desire to see which is the better man. They have fought many times—and they will fight again. Not that the people want to fight, but the Superior Class fan fright into fury, and make men think they must fight to protect their homes.

"So the people who wish to follow the teachings of Christ are not allowed to do so, but are taxed, outraged, deceived by governments.

"Christ taught humility, meekness, the forgiveness of one's enemies, and that to kill was wrong. The Bible teaches men not to swear, but the Superior Class swear us on the Bible in which they do not believe.

"The question is, How are we to relieve ourselves of these cormorants who toil not, but who are clothed in broadcloth and blue, with brass buttons and many costly accoutrements; who feed upon our substance, and for whom we delve and dig?

" Shall we fight them ?

" No, we do not believe in bloodshed ; and besides that, they have the guns and the money, and they can hold out longer than we.

" But who composes this army that they would order to fire upon us ?

" Why, our neighbours and brothers— deceived into the idea that they are doing God's service by protecting their country from its enemies. When the fact is, our country has no enemies save the Superior Class, that pretends to look out for our interests if we will only obey and consent to be taxed.

" Thus do they siphon our resources and turn our true brothers upon us to subdue and humiliate us. You cannot send a telegram to your wife, nor an express package to your friend, nor draw a cheque for your grocer until you first pay the tax to maintain armed men, who can quickly be used to kill you ; and who surely will imprison you if you do not pay.

" The only relief lies in education. Educate men that it is wrong to kill. Teach them the Golden Rule, and yet again teach them the Golden Rule. Silently defy this Superior Class by refusing to bow down to their fetich of bullets. Cease supporting the preachers who cry for war, and spout patriotism for a consideration. Let them go to work as we do. We believe in Christ—they do not. Christ spoke what He thought ; they speak what they think will please the men in power—the Superior Class.

"We will not enlist. We will not shoot on their order. We will not 'charge bayonet' upon a mild and gentle people. We will not fire upon shepherds and farmers, fighting for their firesides, upon suggestion of Cecil Rhodes. Your false cry of 'Wolf, wolf,' shall not alarm us. We pay your taxes only because we have to, and we will pay no longer than we have to. We will pay no pew-rents, no tithes to your sham charities, and we will speak our minds upon occasion.

"We will educate men.

"And all the time our silent influence will be going out, and even the men who are conscripted will be half-hearted and refuse to fight. We will educate men into the thought that the Christ Life of Peace and Good-will is better than the Life of Strife, Bloodshed, and War.

"'Peace on earth!'—it can only come when men do away with armies, and are willing to do unto other men as they would be done by."

So writes a citizen of the United States; and from various sides, in various forms, such voices are sounding.

This is what a German soldier writes:—

"I went through two campaigns with the Prussian Guards (in 1866 and 1870), and I hate war from the bottom of my soul, for it has made me inexpressibly unfortunate. We wounded soldiers generally receive such a miserable recompense that we have indeed to be ashamed of having once been patriots. I, for instance, get ninepence a day for my right arm, which was shot through at the attack on St. Privat, 18th August 1870. Some hunting dogs have more allowed for their keep. And I had suffered for years from my twice wounded arm. Already, in 1866, I took part in the war against Austria, and fought at Trautenau and Königgrätz, and saw horrors enough. In 1870, being in the reserve, I was called out again; and, as I have already said, I was wounded in the attack at St. Privat: my right arm was twice shot through lengthwise. I had to leave a good place in a brewery, and was unable afterwards to regain it. Since then I have never been able to get on my feet again. My intoxication soon passed, and there was nothing left for the wounded invalid but to keep himself alive on a beggarly pittance eked out by charity. . . .

"In a world in which people run round like trained animals, and are not capable of any other idea than that of over-reaching one another for the sake of mammon,—in such a world let people think me a crank; but, for all that, I feel in myself the divine idea of peace, which is so beautifully expressed in the Sermon on the Mount. My deepest conviction is that war is only trade on a larger scale— trade carried on by the ambitious and the powerful with the happiness of the peoples.

"And what horrors do we not suffer

from it! Never shall I forget those
pitiful groans that pierced one to the
marrow!

"People who never did each other any
harm begin to slaughter one another like
wild animals, and petty slavish souls im-
plicate the good God, making Him their
confederate in such deeds.

"My neighbour in the ranks had his
jaw broken by a bullet. The poor wretch
went wild with pain. He ran like a
madman, and in the scorching summer
heat could not even get water to cool his
horrible wound. Our commander, the
Crown Prince (who was afterwards the
noble Emperor Frederick), wrote in his
diary: 'War—is an irony on the Gospels.' . . ."

People are beginning to understand the
fraud of patriotism, in which all the
governments take such pains to keep
them.

CHAPTER VIII

"But," it is usually asked, "what will
there be instead of governments?"

There will be nothing. Something that
has long been useless and therefore superfluous and bad will be abolished. An
organ that, being unnecessary had become
harmful, will be abolished.

"But," people generally say, "if there is no government, people will violate and kill each other."

Why? Why should the abolition of the organisation which arose in consequence of violence, and which traditionally has been handed down from generation to generation to do violence,—why should the abolition of such an organisation, now devoid of use, cause people to outrage and kill one another? On the contrary, the presumption is that the abolition of the organ of violence would result in people ceasing to violate and kill one another.

Now, some men are specially educated and trained to kill and to do violence to other people,—there are men who are supposed to have a right to use violence, and who make use of an organisation which exists for that purpose. Such deeds of violence and such killing are considered good and worthy deeds.

But then, people will not be so educated, and no one will have a right to use violence to others, and there will be no organisation to do violence, and, as is natural to people of our time, violence and murder will always be considered bad actions, no matter who commits them.

But should acts of violence continue to be committed even after the abolition of the governments, still such acts will certainly be fewer than are committed now while an organisation exists specially de-

vised to commit acts of violence, and a
state of things exists in which acts of
violence and murders are considered good
and useful deeds.

The abolition of governments will merely
rid us of an unnecessary organisation which
we have inherited from the past for the
commission of violence and for its justification.

"But there will then be no laws, no
property, no courts of justice, no police,
no popular education," say people who
intentionally confuse the use of violence
by governments with various social activities.

The abolition of the organisation of
government formed to do violence, does
not at all involve the abolition of what is
reasonable and good, and therefore not
based on violence, in laws or law courts,
or in property, or in police regulations, or
in financial arrangements, or in popular
education.   On the contrary, the absence
of the brutal power of government, which
is needed only for its own support, will
facilitate a more just and reasonable social
organisation, needing no violence.   Courts
of justice, and public affairs, and popular
education, will all exist to the extent to
which they are really needed by the
people, but in a shape which will not
involve the evils contained in the present
form of government.   What will be
destroyed is merely what was evil and
hindered the free expression of the
people's will.

But even if we assume that with the absence of governments there would be disturbances and civil strife, even then the position of the people would be better than it is at present. The position now is such that it is difficult to imagine anything worse. The people are ruined, and their ruin is becoming more and more complete. The men are all converted into war-slaves, and have from day to day to expect orders to go to kill and to be killed. What more? Are the ruined peoples to die of hunger? That is already beginning in Russia, in Italy, and in India. Or are the women as well as the men to go to be soldiers? In the Transvaal even that has begun.

So that even if the absence of government really meant Anarchy, in the negative, disorderly sense of that word,—which it is far from meaning,—even in that case, no anarchical disorder could be worse than the position to which governments have already led their peoples, and to which they are leading them.

And therefore emancipation from patriotism, and the destruction of the despotism of government that rests upon it, cannot but be beneficial to mankind.

CHAPTER IX

MEN, recollect yourselves! And for the sake of your well-being, physical and spiritual, for the sake of your brothers and sisters, pause, consider, and think of what you are doing!

Reflect, and you will understand that your foes are not the Boers, or the English, or the French, or the Germans, or the Fins, or the Russians, but that your foes —your only foes—are you yourselves, who maintain by your patriotism the governments that oppress you and make you unhappy.

They have undertaken to protect you from danger, and they have brought that pseudo-protection to such a point that you have all become soldiers, slaves, and are all ruined, or are being ruined more and more, and at any moment may and should expect that the tight-stretched cord will snap, and a horrible slaughter of you and your children will commence.

And however great that slaughter may be, and however that conflict may end, the same state of things will go on. In the same way, and with yet greater intensity, the governments will arm, and ruin, and pervert you and your children, and no one will help you to stop it or to prevent it, if you do not help yourselves.

And there is only one kind of help possible—it lies in the abolition of that terrible linking up into that cone of violence, which enables the person or persons who succeed in seizing the apex, to have power over all the rest, and to hold that power the more firmly the more cruel and inhuman they are, as we see by the cases of the Napoleons, Nicholas I., Bismarck, Chamberlain, Rhodes, and our Russian Dictators who rule the people in the Tsar's name.

And there is only one way to destroy this binding together—it is by shaking off the hypnotism of patriotism.

Understand that all the evils from which you suffer, you yourselves cause by yielding to the suggestions by which emperors, kings, members of parliament, governors, officers, capitalists, priests, authors, artists, and all who need this fraud of patriotism in order to live upon your labour, deceive you!

Whoever you may be, — Frenchman, Russian, Pole, Englishman, Irishman, or Bohemian,—understand that all your real human interests, whatever they may be,— agricultural, industrial, commercial, artistic, or scientific,—as well as your pleasures and joys, in no way run counter to the interests of other peoples or states; and that you are united — by mutual co-operation, by interchange of services, by the joy of wide brotherly intercourse, and by the interchange not merely of goods but also of thoughts and feelings—with the folk of other lands.

Understand that the question, who manages to seize Wei-hai-wei, Port Arthur, or Cuba,—your government or another,—

does not affect you, or rather every such
seizure made by your government injures
you because it inevitably brings in its
train all sorts of pressure on you by your
government, to force you to take part in
the robbery and violence by which alone
such seizures are made, or can be retained
when made. Understand that your life
can in no way be bettered by Alsace becoming German or French, and Ireland or
Poland being free or enslaved; whoever
holds them, you are free to live where you
will, if even you be an Alsatian, an Irishman, or a Pole, yet understand that by
stirring up patriotism you will only make
the case worse; for the subjection in
which your people are kept has resulted
simply from the struggle between patriot-
isms, and every manifestation of patriotism
in one nation provokes a counteracting re-
action in another. Understand that salvation from your woes is only possible when
you free yourself from the obsolete idea
of patriotism and from the obedience to
governments that is based upon it, and
when you boldly enter into the region of
that higher idea, the brotherly union of
the peoples, which has long since come
to life, and from all sides is calling you to
itself.

If people would but understand that
they are not the sons of some fatherland
or other, nor of governments, but are
sons of God, and can therefore neither be
slaves nor enemies one to another, those
insane, unnecessary, worn-out, pernicious

organisations called governments, and all
the sufferings, violations, humiliations,
and crimes which they occasion, would
cease.

PIROGÓVA, 23*rd May* 1900.

[A portion of the translation of this article appeared
contemporaneously in *Reynold's Newspaper*. It is
now first issued complete, translated directly from
the MS.—ED.]

PRINTED BY
MORRISON AND GIBB LIMITED
EDINBURGH

Letters on War

By Leo Colstoy

The Free Age Press
1900

The Free Age Press stands for an attempt to assist in spreading those deep convictions in which the noblest spirits of every age and race have united—that man's true aim and happiness is "unity in reason and love"; the realisation of the brotherhood of all men,—and that we *must* all strive to purge away, each from himself, those false ideas, false feelings, and false desires, personal, social, religious, political, racial, economic, which alienate us one from another and produce nine-tenths of the sum of human suffering.

Of these truly Christian and universally religious aspirations the writings of Leo Tolstoy are perhaps to-day the most definite expression, and it is to the production of 1d., 3d., and 6d. editions of all his known religious, social, and ethical works, together with the unpublished matter and future writings to which we have and shall have special access (being in close relationship with Tolstoy), that *The Free Age Press* will at first devote itself; trusting that all who sympathise will assist by every means in their power, especially in helping to spread the books the world over, losing no opportunity of introducing them whenever and wherever feasible, and of so making it possible for the work to be continued, and extended into wider and wider fields. As it is Tolstoy's desire that his books shall not be copyrighted, our editions will, whenever possible, be free to the world.

Suggestions, criticisms, inquiries, offers of help and co-operation will be gratefully welcomed; and it is specially requested that the names of any books that have helped towards a better understanding of life may be furnished, so that a much needed list may be compiled and published.

Letters, Private Orders, and Money Orders (it is hoped that friends will *purchase* as many copies as possible: even one will help) should be addressed to THE EDITORS, "FREE AGE PRESS," MALDON, ESSEX. *Booksellers* must order from Messrs. SIMPKIN, MARSHALL, HAMILTON, KENT, & Co. LTD., London, E.C.; THE CLARION CO. LTD., 72 Fleet Street, E.C.; Messrs. JOHN MENZIES & Co., Glasgow; Messrs. JOHN HEYWOOD, Manchester,

LETTERS ON WAR

LETTERS
ON WAR

By LEO .
TOLSTOY

THE FREE AGE PRESS

MALDON, ESSEX . . . .

1900

LETTERS ON WAR

———◆———

CAUSES OF THE TRANSVAAL WAR—TWO
WARS—CARTHARGO DELENDA EST—
TO A NON-COMMISSIONED OFFICER

Causes of the Transvaal War

I CANNOT agree with those who attribute
the cause of the present war to the behaviour of this or that political leader.

If two men get drunk in a public-house
and fight whilst playing cards, I cannot
possibly take upon myself to condemn
either, however convincing may be the
arguments of the other. The cause of their
offensive conduct does not by any means
lie in the fact that one of them is right;
but in the fact that, instead of quietly
working and resting, they found fit to
drink wine and play cards in a public-house.

Precisely in the same way, when I am
told that in any given war which has
broken out one side only is to blame, I can
never agree with this. It may be admitted
that one side is behaving worse than the
other, but no investigations as to which
side is behaving worse will in any way

5

explain the cause, owing to which such a terrible, cruel, and inhuman phenomenon as war is taking place.

To anyone who does not shut his eyes, the real causes are perfectly evident in regard to the present Transvaal War, as well as to all the wars which have lately taken place.   These causes are threefold : firstly, the unequal distribution of property, that is, the robbing of one part of humanity by the other; secondly, the existence of the military class of men educated and fore-appointed to murder; and thirdly, the fallacious and, for the most part, fraudulent religious teaching, in which our young generations are forcibly educated. Therefore I think that it is not only useless but harmful to attribute the causes of wars to Chamberlains, William II.'s, and such like; thus hiding from oneself the true causes, which lie much nearer, and in which we are ourselves participating. Chamberlains and Williams we can only rage against and abuse; but our rage and our abuse will only poison our own blood without changing the course of events; for Chamberlains and Williams are but the blind tools of forces lying far behind them. They act as they are obliged to, and they cannot act otherwise.   All history is a series of actions on the part of politicians—exactly similar to those which preceded the Transvaal War; and therefore it is utterly useless, even impossible to be angry with such men and to condemn them, when one sees the true causes of their behaviour, and when one recognises one's own participation in one or other aspect of their activity, according to one's relation to the three fundamental causes I have mentioned.

So long as we will profit by privileged wealth, whilst the masses of the people are crushed with labour, there will always be wars for markets, gold mines, etc., which we require in order to maintain our privileged wealth. So much the more will wars be inevitable whilst we participate in the military organisation, allowing it to exist, and refraining from combating it with all our power. We ourselves either serve in the army or recognise it as being not only indispensable, but praiseworthy; and then when war breaks out, we condemn some Chamberlain or other. But, above all, war will exist so long as we not only profess, but tolerate without anger and indignation that distortion of Christianity which is called the Christian Church, and according to which such things are admissible as a Christ-loving army, the consecration of guns and the recognition of a Christian and righteous war. We teach our children this religion, we profess it ourselves, and then we say—some, that Chamberlain, others, that Kruger is to blame for the murder of men by each other.

These are the reasons why I cannot agree with you and cannot rebuke the blind tools of ignorance and evil, but see the cause of war in a region in which

I can myself contribute either to the diminution or augmentation of the evil. To contribute to the fraternal equalisation of property, to take advantage to the least possible extent of the privileges which have fallen to my lot; to refrain from in any way participating in military activity, to destroy the spell which makes men, whilst becoming hired murderers, imagine that they are acting well by serving in the army; and, above all, to profess the rational Christian teaching, and to endeavour with all one's might to destroy that cruel fraud of false Christianity in which young generations are forcibly educated,—in this threefold work, as it seems to me, consists the duty of every man who wishes to serve that which is right, and who is justly revolted by the present dreadful war.

(A portion of the above appeared first in *Regnolds'*.)

Two Wars

Christendom has recently been the scene of two wars. One is now concluded, whereas the other still continues; but they were for a time being carried on simultaneously, and the contrast they present is very striking. The first—the Spanish and American War—was an old, vain, foolish, and cruel war, inopportune, out-of-date, heathen, which sought by killing one set of people to solve the question as to how and by whom another set of people ought to be governed. The other, which is still going on, and will

end only when there is an end of all war,
is a new, self-sacrificing, holy war, founded
entirely on love and reason, which was
long ago proclaimed (as Victor Hugo
expressed it at one of the congresses) by
the best and most advanced—Christian—
section of mankind against the other, the
coarse and savage section.   This war has
recently been carried on with especial
vigour and success by a handful of
Christian people—the Doukhobortsi of
the Caucasus — against the powerful
Russian Government.

The other day I received a letter from
a gentleman in Colorado—Jesse Glodwin
—who asks me to send him ". . . a few
words or thoughts expressive of my feelings with regard to the noble work of the
American nation, and the heroism of its
soldiers and sailors."   This gentleman,
together with an overwhelming majority
of the American people, feels perfectly
confident that the work of the Americans
—the killing of several thousands of
almost unarmed men (for, in comparison
with the equipment of the Americans, the
Spaniards were almost without arms)—
was beyond doubt a "noble work"; and
he regards the majority of those who,
after killing great numbers of their fellow-
creatures, have remained safe and sound,
and have secured for themselves an
advantageous position, as heroes.

The Spanish-American War — leaving
out of account the atrocities committed
by the Spaniards in Cuba, which served

as a pretext for it—is very like this: An
old man, infirm and childish, brought up
in the traditions of a false honour, chal-
lenges, for the settlement of some misunderstanding, a young man, in full
possession of his powers, to a boxing
match. And the young man, who, from
his antecedents and professed sentiments,
ought to be immeasurably above such a
settlement of the question, accepts the
challenge. Armed with a *casse-tête*, he
then throws himself upon this infirm and
childish old man, knocks out his teeth,
breaks his ribs, and afterwards enthusi-
astically relates his great deeds to a large
audience of young men like himself, who
rejoice and praise the hero who has thus
maimed the old man.

Such is the nature of the first war,
which is occupying the attention of the
whole Christian world. Of the other no
one speaks; hardly anyone knows about it.

This second war may be described as
follows: The people of every nation are
being deluded by their rulers saying to
them, " You, who are governed by us, are
all in danger of being conquered by other
nations; we are watching over your welfare and safety, and consequently we
demand of you annually some millions of
roubles—the fruit of your labour—to be
used by us in the acquisition of arms,
cannon, powder, and ships for your
defence; we also demand that you yourselves shall enter institutions, organised
by us, where you will become senseless

particles of a huge machine—the army—
which will be under our absolute control.
On entering this army you will cease to
be men with wills of your own; you will
simply do what we require of you. But
what we wish, above all else, is to exer-
cise dominion; the means by which we
dominate is killing, therefore we will
instruct you to kill."

Notwithstanding the obvious absurdity
of the assertion that people are in danger
of being attacked by the governments of
other States; who, in their turn, affirm
that they—in spite of all their desire for
peace—find themselves in precisely the
same danger; notwithstanding the humiliation of that slavery to which men
subject themselves by entering the army;
notwithstanding the cruelty of the work
to which they are summoned, men nevertheless submit to this fraud, give their
money to be used for their own subjugation, and themselves help to enslave
others.

But now there come people who say,
"What you tell us about the danger
threatening us, and about your anxiety to
guard us against it, is a fraud. All the
States are assuring us that they desire peace,
and yet at the same time all are arming
themselves against the others. Moreover,
according to that law, which you yourselves recognise, all men are brothers, and
it makes no difference whether one belongs
to this State or to that; therefore the idea
of our being attacked by other nations,

with which you try to frighten us, has no terrors for us, we regard it as a matter of no importance. The essential thing, however, is that the law given to us by God and recognised even by you who are requiring us to participate in killing, distinctly forbids not killing only, but also every kind of violence. Therefore we cannot, and will not, take part in your preparations for murder, we will give no money for the purpose, and we will not attend the meetings arranged by you with the object of perverting men's minds and consciences, and transforming them into instruments of violence, obedient to any bad man who may choose to make use of them."

This constitutes the second war. It has long been carried on by the best men of the world against the representatives of brute force, and has of late flamed up with special intensity between the Doukhobors and the Russian Government. The Russian Government has made use of all the weapons it had at command —police measures for making arrests, for prohibiting people moving from place to place, for forbidding all intercourse with one another, the interception of letters, espionage, the prohibition to publish in the newspapers information about any and every thing concerning the Doukhobors, calumnies of them printed in the papers, bribery, flogging, imprisonment, exile, and the ruin of families.

The Doukhobors have, on their part, employed their one religious weapon, namely, gentle intelligence and patient firmness; and they say, "One must not obey man rather than God. Therefore, whatever you may do to us, we cannot and will not obey you."

Men praise the heroes of the savage Spanish and American War, who, in their desire to distinguish themselves before the world, and to gain reward and fame, have slain great numbers of men, or have died while engaged in killing their fellow-creatures. But no one speaks, or even knows, about the heroes of the war against war, who—unseen and unheard—have died and are now dying under the rod, in foul prison cells or in painful exile, and who, nevertheless, to the last breath, stand firm by goodness and truth.

I knew tens of these martyrs who have already died, and hundreds more who, scattered all over the world, are still suffering martyrdom for confessing the truth.

I knew Droggin, a peasant-teacher, who was tortured to death in a penal battalion; I knew another, Isyumtcheko (a friend of Droggin), who, after being kept for some time in a penal battalion, was banished to the other end of the world. I knew Olkhovikoff, a peasant who refused military service, and was consequently sent to a penal battalion, and then while on board a steamer which was transporting him into exile, converted Sereda, the soldier who had him in charge. Sereda, on apprehending what Olkhovikoff had said to him as to the sinfulness of military service, went to his superiors and said, like the ancient martyrs, "I do not wish to be among the torturers, let me join the martyrs." And forthwith they began to torture him, sent him to a penal battalion, and afterwards exiled him to the province of Yakutsk. I knew tens of Doukhobors, of whom many have died or become blind, and yet they would not yield to demands which are contrary to the divine law.

The other day I read a letter from a young Doukhobor, who had been sent alone to a regiment stationed in Samarkand. Again, those same demands on the part of the officers, the same threats and entreaties, and always the same simple and irresistible replies: "I cannot do what is opposed to my belief in God."

"Then we will torture you to death."

"That is your business. You do your work, and I will do mine."

And this youth of twenty, forsaken of all, in a strange place, surrounded by men who are hostile to him, in the midst of the rich, the powerful, and the educated, who are concentrating all their energies on the task of bringing him to subjection, does not submit, but still perseveres in his heroic deed.

But men say, "These are useless victims; these people perish, but the order of life will remain the same." This, I believe, is just what was said with regard to the sacrifice of Christ, as well as of all the other martyrs to truth. The

men of our time, especially the learned,
have grown so coarse that they, owing to
their coarseness, are even unable to understand the significance and effect of spiritual
force. A shell of fifty pounds of dynamite,
fired at a crowd of living men—this they
understand and recognise as a force; but
thought, truth which has been realised and
practised in the life, even to martyrdom,
which has now become accessible to
millions—this, according to their conception, is not a force, because it makes
no noise, and one cannot see broken bones
and pools of blood. Learned men (true,
it is those whose learning is misdirected)
are using all the power of erudition to
prove that mankind lives like a herd of
cattle, that man is guided by economic
considerations alone, and that his intellect
is given him merely for amusement. But
governments well know what it is that
rules the world, consequently—guided by
the instinct of self-preservation—they are
undoubtedly chiefly concerned about the
manifestation of spiritual forces; upon
which forces depend their existence or
their ruin.

And this is precisely the reason why all
the energies of the Russian Government
were, and still continue to be, exerted to
render the Doukhobors harmless, to isolate
them, to banish them beyond the frontier.

Notwithstanding all these efforts, however, the struggle of the Doukhobors has
opened the eyes of millions.

I know hundreds of military men, old

and young, who, owing to the persecution of the gentle, industrious Doukhobors, have begun to have doubts as to the legality of the activities. I know people who have, for the first time, begun to meditate on life and the meaning of Christianity, only after seeing or hearing about the life of these people, and the persecutions to which they have been subjected.

And the Government that is tyrannising over millions of people knows this, and feels that it has been struck to the very heart.

Such is the nature of the second war which is being waged in our times, and such are its consequences. And not to the Russian Government alone are these consequences of importance; every government founded upon violence and upheld by armies is wounded in the same way by this weapon. Christ said, "*I have conquered the world.*" And, indeed, He has conquered the world, if men would but learn to believe in the strength of the weapon given by Him.

And this weapon is the obedience of every man to his own reason and conscience. This, indeed, is so simple, so indubitable, and binding upon every man; "You wish to make me a participator in murder; you demand of me money for the preparation of weapons; and want me to take part in the organised assembly of murderers," says the reasonable man—he who has neither sold nor obscured his conscience. "But I profess that law— that which is also professed by you—

which long ago forbade not murder only, but all hostility also; and therefore I cannot obey you."

And it is just by this simple means, and by it alone, that the world is being conquered.

(First issued in *The Clarion*. Revised with the original.)

CARTHARGO DELENDA EST

La Vita Internationale and *L'Humanité Nouvelle* have sent me the following letter:—

"SIR,—With the object of furthering the development of humanitarian ideas and civilisation, *La Vita Internationale* (of Milan), with the support of *L'Humanité Nouvelle* (of Paris and Brussels), has deemed it necessary to interest itself in the difficult problem which has of late arisen in all its gravity and importance, owing to the delicate question about which France and the whole world have become so ardently impassioned—we mean the problem of war and militarism. With this aim in view, we beg all those in Europe who take part in politics, science, art, and the labour movement, and even those who occupy the foremost positions in the army, to contribute to this most civilising task by replying to the following questions:—

"1. Is war among civilised nations still required by history, law, and progress?

"2. What are the intellectual, moral, physical, economical, and political effects of militarism?

2

"3. What, in the interests of the world's future civilisation, are the solutions which should be given to the grave problems of war and militarism?

"What means would most rapidly lead to these solutions?"

I cannot conceal the feelings of disgust, indignation, and even despair which were aroused in me by this letter. Enlightened, sensible, good Christian people who confess the principle of love and brotherhood, who regard murder as an awful crime, who, with very few exceptions, are unable to kill an animal—all these people suddenly, provided that these crimes are called war, not only acknowledge the destruction, plunder, and killing of people to be right and legal, but themselves contribute towards these plunders and murders, prepare themselves for them, take part in them, are proud of them. Moreover, always and everywhere one and the same phenomenon repeats itself, namely, that the great majority of people—all working people—those very people who carry out the plunders and murders, and on whom all the burden falls—neither devise nor prepare nor desire these things, but take part in them against their will, merely because they are placed in such a position and are so instigated that it appears to them, to each individual, that they would suffer more were they to refuse. Whereas those who devise and prepare for these plunders and murders, and who compel the working people to carry them out, are

but an insignificant minority, who live in
luxury and idleness, upon the labour of
the workers. This deceit has already
been going on for a long time, but lately
the insolence of the impostors has reached
its extremest development, and a great
share of what labour produces is being
taken away from the workers and used for
making preparations for plundering and
killing. In all the constitutional countries
of Europe the workers themselves—all,
without exception—are called upon to take
part in these plunders and murders; international relations are purposely always
more and more complicated, and this leads
on to war; peaceful countries are being
plundered without the least cause; every
year, in some place or other, people
murder and rob; and all live in constant
dread of general, mutual robbery and
murder. It seems evident that if these
things are done, it can only be because the
great mass of people are deceived by the
minority to whom this deceit is advantageous, and therefore that the first task
of those who are anxious to free people
from the evils caused by this mutual
murdering and plundering should be to
expose the deception under which the
masses are labouring; to point out to
them how the deceit is perpetrated, by
what means it is being upheld, and how
to get rid of it. The enlightened people
of Europe, however, do nothing of the
kind, but under the pretext of furthering
the establishment of peace, they assemble

now in one, now in another city of Europe,
and, seated at tables, with most serious
faces they discuss the question how best
to persuade those brigands who live by
their plunder to give up robbing and
become peaceful citizens; and then they
put the profound questions: first, whether
war is still desirable from the standpoint
of history, law, and progress (as if such
fictions, invented by us, could demand
from us deviation from the fundamental
moral law of our life); secondly, as to
what are the consequences of war (as if
there could be any doubt that the consequences of war are always general dis-
tress and corruption); and finally, as to
how to solve the problem of war (as if
some difficult problem existed as to how
to free deluded people from a delusion
which we clearly see).

This is terrible! We see, for instance,
how healthy, calm, and frequently happy
people year after year arrive at some
gambling den like Monte Carlo, and, bene-
fiting no one but the keepers of those
dens, leave there their health, peace,
honour, and often their lives. We pity
these people; we see clearly that the
deceit to which they are subjected consists
in those temptations whereby gamblers
are allured; in the inequality of the
chances, and in the infatuation of gamblers
who, though fully aware that in general
they are sure to be losers, nevertheless
hope, for once at least, to be more fortunate than the rest. All this is perfectly

clear. And then, in order to free people
from these miseries, we—instead of point-
ing out to them the temptations to which
they are subjected, the fact that they are
sure to lose, and the immorality of gambling,
which is based on the expectation of other
people's misfortunes—assemble with grave
faces at meetings, and discuss how to
arrange that the keepers of gambling-
houses should, of their own accord, shut
up their establishments; we write books
about it, and we put questions to ourselves
as to whether history, law, and progress
require the existence of gambling-houses,
and as to what are the economical, intellectual, moral, and other consequences of
roulette.

If a man is given to drink, and I tell
him that he himself can leave off drinking
and that he must do so, there is a hope
that he will listen to me; but if I tell him
that his drunkenness is a complicated and
difficult problem which we learned men
are trying to solve at our meetings, then in
all probability he will, while awaiting the
solution of this problem, continue to drink.
Thus also with these false and refined external, scientific means of abolishing war,
such as international tribunals, arbitration,
and similar absurdities, while all the time
carefully omitting to mention the most
simple, essential, and self-evident method of
causing war to cease—a method plain for all
to see. In order that people who do not
want war should not fight, it is not necessary to have either international law, arbi-

tration, international tribunals, or solutions
of problems; but it is merely necessary
that those who are subjected to the deceit
should awaken and free themselves from
the spell or enchantment under which they
find themselves. The way to do away
with war is for those who do not want war,
who regard participation in it as a sin, to
refrain from fighting. This method has
been preached from the earliest times by
Christian writers such as Tertullian and
Origen, as well as by the Paulicians, and
by their successors, the Mennonites,
Quakers, and Herrnhuters. The sin,
harmfulness, and senselessness of military
service have been written about and exposed in every way by Dymond, Garrison,
and, twenty years ago, by Ballou, as well
as by myself. The method I have mentioned has been adopted in the past, and
of late has been frequently resorted to by
isolated individuals in Austria, Prussia,
Holland, Switzerland, and Russia, as well
as by whole societies like the Quakers,
Mennonites, and Nazarenes, and recently
by the Doukhobors, of whom a whole
population of 15,000 for three years re-
sisted the powerful Russian Government,
and, notwithstanding all the sufferings to
which they were subjected, did not submit to its demands that they should take
part in the crimes of military service.

But the enlightened friends of peace not
only refrain from recommending this
method, but cannot bear the mere mention
of it, and when it is brought before them

they pretend not to have noticed it, or, if they cannot help noticing it, they gravely shrug their shoulders and express their pity for those uneducated and unreasonable men who adopt such an ineffectual, silly method, when such a good one exists —namely, to sprinkle salt on the tail of the bird one wishes to catch, *i.e.*, to persuade the governments, who only exist by violence and deceit, to forsake both the one and the other.

They tell us that the misunderstandings which arise between governments will be settled by tribunals or by arbitration. But the governments do not at all desire the settlement of misunderstandings On the contrary, if there be none they invent some, it being only by such misunderstanding with other governments that they are afforded a pretext for keeping up the army upon which their power is based. Thus the enlightened friends of peace strive to divert the attention of the working, suffering masses from the only method that can deliver them from the slavery in which they are held (from their youth upward), first by patriotism, next by oaths administered by the mercenary priests of a perverted Christianity, and, lastly, by the fear of punishment.

In our days of close and peaceful relations between the people of different nationalities and countries, the deceit called patriotism (which always claims the pre-eminence of one State or nationality over the rest, and which is therefore always involving people in useless and pernicious wars) is too evident for reasonable people of our age not to free themselves from it; and the religious deceit of the obligation of the oath (which is distinctly forbidden by that very gospel which the governments profess) is, thank God, ever less and less believed in. So that what really prevents the great majority from refusing to take part in military service is merely fear of the punishments which are inflicted by the governments for such refusals. This fear, however, is only a result of the government deceit, and has no other basis but hypnotism.

The governments may and should fear those who refuse to serve, and, indeed, they are afraid of them, because every refusal undermines the prestige of the deceit by which the governments have the people in their power. But those who refuse have no ground whatever to fear a government that demands crimes from them. In refusing military service, every man risks much less than he would were he to enter it. The refusal of military service and the punishment—imprisonment, exile —is only an advantageous insurance of oneself against the dangers of the military service. In entering the service, every man risks having to take part in war (for which purpose he is being prepared), and during war he may be, like a man sentenced to death, placed in a position in which, under the most difficult and painful circumstances, he will almost certainly be killed or crippled, as I have seen in Sebastopol, when a regiment marched to a fort where two regiments had already been destroyed, and stood there until it too was entirely exterminated. Another, more profitable, chance is that the man who enters the army will not be killed, but will only fall ill and die in the unhealthy conditions of military service. A third chance is that, having been insulted by his superior, he will be unable to contain himself, will answer sharply, will break the discipline, and be subjected to punishment much worse than that to which he would have been liable had he refused military service. The best chance, however, is that instead of the imprisonment or exile to which a person refusing military service is liable, he will pass three or five years of his life amid vicious surroundings, practising the art of killing, being all the while in the same captivity as in prison, and in humiliating submission to depraved people. This in the first place.

Secondly, in refusing military service, every man, however strange it may seem, can yet always hope to escape punishment —upon his refusal being that last disclosure of the governments' deceit, which will render any further punishment for such a deed impossible, there being no people then left sufficiently stupefied to take part in the punishment of one who refuses to participate in their oppression. So that submission to the demands of military service is, evidently, only submission to the hypnotisation of the masses —the utterly futile rush of Panurge's sheep into the water to their evident destruction.

Moreover, besides the consideration of advantage, there is yet another reason which should impel every man to refuse military service who is not hypnotised, and is conscious of the importance of his actions. No one can help desiring that his life should not be an aimless and useless existence, but that it should be of service to God and man; yet frequently a man spends his life without finding an opportunity for such service. The summons to accept the military service presents precisely such an opportunity to every man of our time. Every man, in refusing to take part in military service or to pay taxes to a government which uses them for military purposes, is, by this refusal, rendering a great service to God and man, for he is thereby making use of the most efficacious means of furthering the progressive movement of mankind towards that better social order which it is striving after and must eventually attain. But not only is it advantageous to refuse participation in the military service, and not only should the majority of the men of our time so refuse : it is, moreover, *impossible* not to refuse, if only they are not hypnotised. To every man there are some actions which are morally impossible—as impossible as are certain physical actions. And the promise of slavish obedience to strangers and to immoral people who have the murder of men as their acknowledged object, is, to the majority of men, if only they be free from hypnotism, just such a morally impossible action. And therefore it is not only advantageous and obligatory on every man to refuse to participate in the military service, but it is also impossible for him not to do so if only he be free from the stupefaction of hypnotism.

"But what will happen when all people refuse military service, and there is no check nor hold over the wicked, and the wicked triumph, and there is no protection against savage people—against the yellow race—who will come and conquer us?"

I will say nothing about the fact that as it is the wicked have long triumphed, that they are still triumphing, and that while fighting one another they have long dominated the Christians, so that there is no need to fear what has already been accomplished; nor will I say anything with regard to the dread of the savage yellow race—whom we insistently provoke and instruct in war—that being a mere excuse, and one-hundredth part of the army now kept up in Europe being sufficient for the imaginary protection against them—I will say nothing about all this, because the consideration of the general result to the world of such or such actions cannot serve as a guide for our conduct and activity.

To man is given another guide, and that
an unfailing one,—the guide of his conscience, following which he indubitably
knows that he is doing what he should
do. Therefore, all considerations of the
danger that threatens every individual
who refuses military service, as well as of
what menaces the world in consequence
of such refusals—all these are but a
particle of that enormous and monstrous
deceit in which Christian mankind is
enmeshed, and which is being carefully
maintained| by the governments who
exist by the power of this deceit.

If man act in accordance with what is
dictated to him by his reason, his conscience, and his God, only the very best can
result for himself as well as for the world.

People complain of the evil conditions
of life in our Christian world. But is it
possible for it to be otherwise, when all of
us acknowledge not only that fundamental
Divine law proclaimed some thousands of
years ago, "Thou shalt not kill," but also
the law of love and brotherhood of all
men, and yet, notwithstanding this, every
man in our European world practically
disavows this fundamental Divine law
acknowledged by him, and at the command
of President, Emperor, or Minister, of
Nicholas or William, arrays himself in a
ridiculous costume, takes an instrument of
murder, and says, "Here I am, ready to
injure, ruin, or kill anyone I am ordered
to"?

What must a society be like which is

composed of such men? Such a society must be dreadful, and indeed it is so!

Awake, brethren! Listen neither to those villains who, from your childhood, infect you with the diabolic spirit of patriotism, opposed to righteousness and truth, and only necessary in order to deprive you of your property, your freedom, and your human dignity; nor to those ancient impostors who preach war in the name of a cruel and vindictive God invented by them, and in the name of a perverted and false Christianity; nor, even less, to those modern Sadducees who, in the name of science and civilisation, aiming only at the continuation of the present state of things, assemble at meetings, write books, and make speeches, promising to organise a good and peaceful life for people without their making any effort! Do not believe them. Believe only the consciousness which tells you that you are neither beasts nor slaves, but free men, responsible for your actions, and therefore unable to be murderers either of your own accord or at the will of those who live by these murders. And it is only necessary for you to awake in order to realise all the whole horror and insanity of that which you have been and are doing, and, having realised this, to cease that evil which you yourselves abhor, and which is ruining you. If only you were to refrain from the evil which you yourselves detest, those ruling impostors, who first corrupt and then oppress you, would disappear like owls before the daylight, and then those new, human, brotherly conditions of life would be established for which Christendom—weary of suffering, exhausted by deceit, and lost in insolvable contradictions — is longing. Only let every man without any intricate or sophisticated arguments accomplish that which to-day his conscience unfailingly bids him do, and he will recognise the truth of the gospel words: "If any man willeth to do His will, he shall know of the teaching, whether it be of God, or whether I speak from Myself" (St. John · vii. 17).

(First issued in *Westminster Gazette.* Revised with original.)

To a Non-Commissioned Officer

(*Translated by Aylmer Maude*)

You are surprised that soldiers are taught that it is right to kill people in certain cases and in war, while in the books admitted to be holy by those who so teach, there is nothing like such a permission, but, on the contrary, not only is all murder forbidden, but all insulting of others is forbidden also, and we are told not to do to others what we do not wish done to us. And you ask, is not this a fraud! And if it is a fraud, then for whose sake is it done?

Yes, it is a fraud, committed for the sake of those accustomed to live on the sweat and blood of other men, and who have therefore perverted, and still pervert, Christ's teaching, which was given to man for his good, but which has now, in its perverted form, become the chief source of human misery.

The thing has come about in this way :—

The government, and all those people of the upper classes who are near the government, and who live by the work of others, need some means of dominating the workers, and this means they find in their control of the army. Defence against foreign enemies is only an excuse. The German Government frightens its subjects about the Russians and the French; the French Government frightens its people about the Germans; the Russian Government frightens its people about the French and the Germans, and that is the way with all governments. But neither the Germans nor Russians nor Frenchmen desire to fight their neighbours and other people; but, living in peace, they dread war more than anything else in the world. The government and the upper governing classes, to excuse their domination of the labourers, behave like a gipsy who whips his horse before he turns a corner and then pretends he cannot hold it in. They provoke their own people and some foreign government, and then pretend that for the well-being or for the defence of their people they must declare war, which again brings profit only to generals, officers, officials, merchants, and, in general, to the rich. In reality war is an inevitable result of the existence of armies; and armies are only needed by governments in order to dominate their own working classes.

The thing is a crime, but the worst of it is that the government, in order to have a plausible basis for its domination of the people, has to pretend that it holds the highest religious teaching known to man (*i.e.* the Christian), and that it brings up its subjects in this teaching. That teaching, however, is in its nature opposed not only to murder, but to all violence, and, therefore, the governments, in order to dominate the people and to be considered Christian, had to pervert Christianity and to hide its true meaning from the people, and thus deprive men of the well-being Christ brought them.

This perversion was accomplished long ago, in the time of that scoundrel the Emperor Constantine, who for doing it was enrolled among the saints.[1] All subsequent governments, especially our Russian Government, do their utmost to preserve this perverted understanding, and not to allow the people to see the real meaning of Christianity; because having seen the real meaning of Christianity, the people would perceive that the governments, with their taxes, soldiers, prisons, gallows, and false priests, are not

---

[1] Constantine the Great was decreed to be a god by the Roman Senate, and was made a Christian saint by the Eastern Church.—*Trans.*

only not the pillars of Christianity they profess to be, but are its greatest enemies.

In consequence of this perversion, those frauds which have surprised you are possible, and all those terrible misfortunes occur from which people suffer.

The people are oppressed, robbed, poor, ignorant, dying of hunger. Why? Because the land is in the hands of the rich; the people are enslaved in mills and in factories, obliged to earn money because taxes are demanded from them, and the price of their labour is diminished, while the price of things they need is increased.

How are they to escape? By taking the land from the rich? But if this is done, soldiers will come and will kill the rebels or put them in prison. Take the mills and factories? The same will happen. Organise and support a strike? But it is sure to fail. The rich will hold out longer than the workers, and the armies are always on the side of the capitalists. The people will never extricate themselves from the want in which they are kept, as long as the army is in the hands of the governing classes.

But who compose these armies that keep the people in this state of slavery? Who are these soldiers that will fire at the peasants who take the land, or at the strikers who will not disperse, and at the smugglers who bring in goods without paying taxes, who put in prison and guard there those who refuse to pay taxes? The soldiers are these same peasants who are

3

deprived of land, these same strikers who want better wages, these same taxpayers who want to be rid of these taxes.

And why do these people shoot at their brothers? Because it has been instilled into them that the oath they were obliged to take on entering the service, is binding, and that though it is generally wrong to murder people, it is right to do so at the command of their superiors. That is to say that that fraud is played off upon them which has occurred to you. But here we meet the question, How is it that sensible people—often people who can read, and even educated people—believe in such an evident lie? However little education a man may have, he cannot but know that Christ did not sanction murder, but taught kindness, meekness, forgiveness of injuries, love of one's enemies; and therefore he cannot help seeing that on the basis of Christian teaching he cannot pledge himself in advance to kill all whom he may be ordered to kill.

The question is, How can sensible people believe, as all now serving in the army have believed and still believe, such an evident fraud? The answer is that it is not this one fraud by itself that takes people in, but they have from childhood been deprived of the proper use of their reason by a whole series of frauds, a whole system of frauds, called the Orthodox Faith, which is nothing but the grossest idolatry. In this faith people are taught that God is triple, that besides this triple

God there is a Queen of Heaven,[1] and besides this Queen there are various saints whose corpses have not decayed,[2] and besides these saints there are icons [3] of the Gods and of the Queen of Heaven, to which one should offer candles and pray with one's hands; and that the most important and holy thing on earth is the pap,[4] which the parson makes of wine and white bread on Sundays behind a railing; and that after the parson has whispered over it, the wine is no longer wine, and the white bread is not bread, but they are the blood and flesh of one of the triple Gods, etc. All this is so stupid and senseless that it is quite impossible to under-

[1] The Holy Virgin, the "Mother of God" and "Queen of Heaven," plays a prominent part in the Orthodox Eastern Church, *i.e.* the Russo - Greek Church.—*Trans.*

[2] One proof of holiness adduced as justifying admission to the rank of sainthood is the non-decomposition of the holy person's corpse. These miraculously preserved bodies are enshrined in chapels, monasteries, and cathedrals, and are there visited by pilgrims, who offer up prayers at the shrine, place candles before it, and usually leave some contribution for the benefit of the establishment. The inspection allowed is not very close, and there are stories of people being employed to stuff the saints with straw. These tales are, however, considered irreligious.—*Trans.*

[3] The icons of the Eastern Church are not "graven images," but are pictures painted in a conventional cadaverous manner on wood; these are often covered with an embossed metal cover allowing only the hands and face to be seen, and making the icon as much like an image as a picture.—*Trans.*

[4] "The pap" is the author's irreverent way of referring to the mixture of bread and wine administered by the priests of the Orthodox Eastern Church at the celebration of the Holy Eucharist.—*Trans.*

stand what it all means. And the very
people who teach this faith don't tell you
to understand it, but only tell you to
believe it; and people trained to it from
childhood can believe any kind of nonsense that is told them. And when men
have been so befooled that they believe
that God hangs in the corner,[1] or sits in
a morsel of pap which the parson gives
out in a spoon; that to kiss a board or
some relic, and to put candles in front of
them, is useful for life here and hereafter,
—they are called on to enter the military
service, where they are humbugged to any
extent, being made to swear on the Gospel
(in which swearing is prohibited) that they
will do just what is forbidden in those
Gospels, and then taught that to kill
people at the word of those in command
is not a sin, but that to refuse to submit
to those in command is a sin. So that
the fraud played off on soldiers, when it
is instilled into them that they may without sin kill people at the wish of those in
command, is not an isolated fraud, but is
bound up with a whole system of fraud,
without which this one fraud would not
deceive them.

Only a man who is quite befooled by
the false faith called Orthodoxy, palmed
off upon him for the true Christian faith,
can believe that there is no sin in a

---

[1] This refers to the common practice of hanging
an icon in the corner of each dwelling-room. These
icons are called "gods," and are prayed to in a
way that among common and devout people often
amounts to idolatry.—*Trans.*

Christian entering the army, promising blindly to obey any man who ranks above him in the service, and, at the will of others, learning to kill, and committing that most terrible crime, forbidden by all laws.

A man free from the pseudo-Christian faith called Orthodoxy will not believe that.

And that is why the so-called Sectarians, *i.e.* Christians who have repudiated the Orthodox teaching and acknowledge Christ's teaching as explained in the Gospels, and especially in the Sermon on the Mount, are not tricked by this deception, but have frequently refused, and still do refuse, to be soldiers, considering such occupation incompatible with Christianity, and preferring to bear all kinds of persecution, as hundreds and thousands of people are doing: in Russia among the Doukhobors and Molokans, in Austria the Nazarenes, and in Sweden, Switzerland, and Germany among members of the Evangelical sects. The government knows this, and is therefore exceedingly anxious that the general Church fraud, without which its power could not be maintained, should be commenced with every child from early infancy, and should be continually maintained in such a way that none may avoid it. The government tolerates anything else, drunkenness and vice (and not only tolerates but even organises drunkenness and vice — they help to stupefy people),—but by all the

means in its power it hinders those who
have escaped from its trap from assisting
others to escape.

The Russian Government perpetrates
this fraud with special craft and cruelty.
It orders all its subjects to baptize their
children during infancy into the false faith
called Orthodoxy, and it threatens to punish
them if they disobey.   And when the
children are baptized, *i.e.* are reckoned as
Orthodox, then under threats of criminal
penalties they are forbidden to discuss the
faith into which, without their wish, they
were baptized; and for such discussion of
that faith, as well as for renouncing it
and passing to another, they are actually
punished.   So that about all Russians it
cannot be said that they believe the
Orthodox faith, — they do not know
whether they believe it or not, but were
converted to it during infancy and kept in
it by violence, *i.e.* by the fear of punishment.   All Russians were entrapped into
Orthodoxy by a cunning fraud, and are
kept in it by cruel force.

Using the power it wields, the government perpetrates and maintains this fraud,
and the fraud upholds its power.

And, therefore, the sole means to free
people from their many miseries lies in
freeing them from the false faith instilled
into them by government, and in their
imbibing the true Christian teaching
which is hidden by this false teaching.
The true Christian teaching is very simple,
clear, and obvious to all, as Christ said.

But it is simple and accessible only when man is freed from that falsehood in which we were all educated, and which is passed off upon us as God's Truth.

Nothing needful can be poured into a vessel full of what is useless. We must first empty out what is useless. So it is with the acquirement of true Christian teaching. We have first to understand that all the stories telling how God six thousand years ago made the world; how Adam sinned and the human race fell, and how the Son of God, a God born of a virgin, came on earth and redeemed man, and all the fables in the Old Testament and in the Gospels, and all the lives of the saints with their stories of miracles and relics, are nothing but a gross hash of Jewish superstitions and priestly frauds. Only to a man quite free from this deception can the clear and simple teaching of Christ, which needs no explanation, be accessible and comprehensible. That teaching tells us nothing of the beginning, or of the end, of the world, nor about God and His purpose, nor in general about things which we cannot, and need not, know; but it speaks only of what man must do to save himself, *i.e.* how best to live the life he has come into, in this world, from birth to death. For this purpose it is only necessary to act to others as we wish them to act to us. In that is all the law and the prophets, as Christ said. And to act in that way we need neither icons, nor relics, nor church services, nor priests, nor catechisms, nor governments, but, on the contrary, we need perfect freedom from all that; for to do to others as we wish them to do to us is only possible when a man is free from the fables which the priests give out as the only truth, and is not bound by promises to act as other people may order. Only such a man will be capable of fulfilling—not his own will nor that of other men—but the will of God.

And the will of God is not that we should fight and oppress the weak, but that we should acknowledge all men to be our brothers, and should serve one another.

These are the thoughts your letter has aroused in me. I shall be very glad if they help to clear up the questions you are thinking about.

(Reprinted from *The New Order*.)

PRINTED BY
MORRISON AND GIBB LIMITED, EDINBURGH

THREEPENCE

Thoughts
on God

By Leo
Tolstoy

The Free Age Press
1900

The Free Age Press stands for an attempt to assist in spreading those deep convictions in which the noblest spirits of every age and race have united—that man's true aim and happiness is "unity in reason and love"; the realisation of the brotherhood of all men,—and that we *must* all strive to purge away, each from himself, those false ideas, false feelings, and false desires, personal, social, religious, political, racial, economic, which alienate us one from another and produce nine-tenths of the sum of human suffering.

Of these truly Christian and universally religious aspirations the writings of Leo Tolstoy are perhaps to-day the most definite expression, and it is in the production of 1d., 3d., and 6d. editions of all his known religious, social, and ethical works, together with the unpublished matter and future writings to which we have and shall have special access (being in close relationship with Tolstoy) that *The Free Age Press* will at first devote itself, trusting that all who sympathise will assist by every means in their power, especially in helping to spread the books the world over, losing no opportunity of introducing them whenever and wherever feasible, and of so making it possible for the work to be continued, and extended into wider and wider fields. As it is Tolstoy's desire that his books shall not be copyrighted, our editions will, whenever possible, be free to the world.

Suggestions, criticisms, inquiries, offers of help and co-operation will be gratefully welcomed, and it is specially requested that the names of any books that have helped towards a better understanding of life may be furnished, so that a much needed list may be compiled and published.

Letters, Private Orders, and Money Orders (it is hoped that friends will *purchase* as many copies as possible : even one will help) should be addressed to THE EDITORS, " FREE AGE PRESS," MALDON, ESSEX. *Booksellers* must order from Messrs. SIMPKIN, MARSHALL, HAMILTON, KENT & CO. LTD., London, E.C. ; THE CLARION LTD., 72 Fleet Street, E.C. ; Messrs. JOHN MENZIES & CO., Glasgow ; and Mr. JOHN HEYWOOD, Manchester.

THOUGHTS ON GOD

NOTE TO SECOND EDITION

THE reader may be interested in knowing the author's own impression of these "Thoughts" when reading them in the first edition of this booklet, published a considerable time after its contents were written. In a private letter, dated 6th September 1900, he says: "I have just read 'Thoughts on God.' There is in them that which is good, and I was moved in reading. But their publication is premature. They should have been published after my death (not distant). Otherwise, it is fearful to live with such a life-programme. — These were my first thoughts on reading; and then I was ashamed of myself. If one lives not before men but before God, is not the publication of one's beliefs immaterial? To live before men is very troublesome; to satisfy everyone, earn everyone's good opinion, conceal one's foulness—is very difficult. But how peaceful and easy to live before God. Before Him one need not trouble to dissimulate or pose. He knows what one is, and what one is worth. This alone is one—and a great—advantage of serving God and not men.

"Also, whilst reading, I recalled to mind that which lately I have been thinking—that one cannot say, God is Love, or God is Logos, Reason. Through Love and Reason we indeed apprehend God; but these ideas not only do not cover the idea of God—they differ from it as much as the idea of an eye or of sight differs from the light itself.

"Almost the same thing is said in the booklet."

THOUGHTS

ON GOD .

By LEO .
TOLSTOY

THE FREE AGE PRESS
CHRISTCHURCH, HANTS . .
(New Address)

1900

TRANSLATOR'S NOTE

THE thoughts here offered to the reader, illustrating what Leo Tolstoy understands by the term " God," have been extracted from his diaries, private letters, note-book jottings, draught manuscripts of unfinished papers, and various writings of the same kind. A portion of the matter has already appeared ; the remainder has not been published before. If the reader desires to form a complete idea of Tolstoy's views on this subject, he should supplement these thoughts by what the author has written on the same theme in his previously published works and in the other booklets in this series.

The reader is requested to bear in mind that the thoughts here presented, not being originally intended by the author for publication, are not expressed as precisely and carefully as they would have been had he been preparing them for the general public ; and also that the translation of writings of this character affords special difficulties, owing to their rough and unfinished form.

In order, therefore, that the reader may both do justice to these expressions of thought and fully profit by them, it is desirable that he should endeavour to understand any verbal imperfections according to the spirit of the whole, and to fill up in the sense most advantageous for the thought expressed, any omission he may remark. V. T.

THOUGHTS ON GOD

———◆———

GOD is for me that after which I strive
—that, in striving after which consists
my life, and who therefore for me *is*;
but is necessarily such that I cannot
comprehend or name Him. If I understood Him, I should have reached Him,
and there would be nothing to strive
after; there would be no life. But,
and this seems a contradiction, though
I cannot understand nor name Him,
yet at the same time I know Him and
the direction towards Him, and even of
all my knowledge this is the most
certain.

I do not comprehend Him, yet at
the same time I am always anxious
when I am without Him, and am not
anxious only when I am with Him.
What is still more strange is that to
know Him more and better than I do
at present is not my desire now in this
present life, and is not necessary. I
can draw nearer to Him, and I wish to

do so;—in that is my life; but such drawing nearer in no way increases, and cannot increase, my knowledge.

Every endeavour of the imagination to know Him more definitely (for instance, as my Creator, or as a Merciful Being) removes me farther from Him, and prevents me drawing nearer to Him.

Stranger still, I can love truly—that is, more than myself or than anything else — Him alone. This love alone knows no check, no decrease (on the contrary, all is increase), no sensuality, no insincerity, no subserviency, no fear, no self-satisfaction. Only through this love does one love all that is good; so that one loves and lives only through Him and by Him.

Well, this is how I think, or rather feel. I have only to add that the pronoun " He " somewhat destroys my idea of God: the word " He " somewhat diminishes Him.

. . . . . .

It is astonishing how I could formerly fail to see the indubitable truth, that behind this world and our life in it, is someone, something, that knows why this world exists and why we, in it, like bubbles in boiling water, rise, burst, and disappear.

It is certain that something is being done in this world, and that by all

living beings; being done by me, by
my life. Otherwise, wherefore this
sun, these seasons, and above all,
wherefore this three - year - old child,
frenzièd with superabundance of life;
that old woman who has outlived her
reason; or yonder lunatic? These
separate beings, which in my eyes
evidently have no meaning, and which
are yet living so vigorously, are so
tenacious of life, and in whom life is so
firmly planted, these beings more than
anything convince me that they are
wanted for some purpose that is wise
and good, and inaccessible to me.

. . . . .

Why are you downcast? You are
waiting for something too great—waiting, it seems to me, for God in thunder
and storm, and not in stillness. The
best of it is that, as you say, you cannot
"get away anywhere." In this the
hand of God is most visible and palpable.

You say that I do not seem to acknowledge God. This is a misunderstanding. I acknowledge nothing but
God.

I think I wrote and spoke to you
about my definition of God, which I
would now give in answer to the question, What is God? *God is that All,
that infinite All, of which I am conscious of being a part, and therefore all*

in me is encompassed by God, and I feel Him in everything.

And this is not at all a play of words; it is that by which I live.

.　　.　　.　　.

What is God? Wherefore God?

God is that *un*limited *all* which. I know within myself in a limited form. I am limited, God is infinite; I am a being which has lived sixty-three years, God lives eternally; I am a being which reasons within the limits of its understanding, God reasons without limit; I am a being which loves sometimes a little, God loves always infinitely. I am a part, He is all. I cannot understand myself otherwise than as a part of Him.

.　　.　　.　　.

Somehow, while praying to God, it became clear to me that God is indeed a real Being, Love,—is that All which I just touch, and which I experience in the form of love. And this is not a feeling, not an abstraction, but a real Being; and I have felt Him.

.　　.　　.　　.

All that I know, I know because there is a God, and because I know Him. Only upon this can one firmly base one's relations, both with other men and with oneself, as well as with life outside space and time. Not only do I not regard this as mystical, but

I hold the opposite view to be mystical;
whereas this is the most intelligible
and accessible reality.

.   .   .   .   .

To the definition of God I find it
necessary to add that of Matthew
Arnold, which I have kept in mind
as expressing one aspect, and that the
chief, in which God presents Himself
to us. (Matthew Arnold deduces his
definition from the Old Testament prophets, and, indeed, for the time previous
to Christ, it is sufficiently complete.)
God is that eternal, infinite, "not ourselves" which "makes for righteousness." One may call it the law of
human life, the will of God in relation
to that part of men's life which is in
their power. I say that this definition
was sufficient up to the time of Christ,
but by Christ it has been revealed to
us that the fulfilment of this law,
besides its external obligation to
human reason, has also another and
more simple inner motive which pene-
trates all man's being; namely, love:
love, not of wife, or child, or country,
but love of God (God is Love), love of
love—that same feeling of kindness,
sympathy, and joy of life, which constitutes man's natural, blissful, true
life which knows no death.

.   .   .   .   .

One knows God, not so much through

reason, nor even through the heart, but through one's feeling of complete dependence on Him, akin to the feeling experienced by an unweaned child in the arms of its mother. It does not know who holds it, warms it, feeds it; but it knows that there is this someone; and more than knows—it loves that being.

.   .   .   .   .

Formerly I witnessed the phenomena of life without thinking whence they came, or why I witnessed them.

Subsequently I realised that all that I see is the outcome of light, which is understanding. And I was so glad to have brought everything into harmony, that I was quite satisfied in acknowledging the understanding alone to be the source of everything.

But after that I saw that the understanding is a light which reaches me through a kind of dim glass. I see the light, but its source I do not know. Yet I know that the source exists.

This same source, which is the source of the light that enlightens me—a source I do not know, but the existence of which I do know—is God.

.   .   .   .   .

To love means to desire that which the one we love desires. But men desire opposite things, whereas that only can be loved which desires one and the same thing. One and the same thing is desired only by God.

To love God means to desire that which He desires. And He desires universal welfare.

"Brethren, let us love one another. He that loveth is born of God and knoweth God, because (it is written 'God is Love,' but we ought to say) Love is God." But also God is love, *i.e.* we know God only in the form of love, and love is God, *i.e.* if we love we are not God's but God.

Yes, love is God.

Love — love him who has caused thee pain, whom thou hast blamed, disliked; and then all that which had concealed his soul from thee will disappear, and thou wilt, as through clear water, see at the bottom of his soul the divine essence of his love; and thou wilt not have to, thou wilt not be able to pardon him; thou wilt only have to pardon thyself for not having loved God in him in whom He was, and for not having seen Him through the absence of thy love.

Love is the manifestation within oneself (the consciousness) of God, and therefore the propensity to get out of oneself, to liberate oneself, to live a

godly life. And this propensity calls
forth God, *i.e.* Love in others.

This is not expressed clearly.

My chief idea is that love evokes
love in others. God, having awakened
in me, produces the awakening of the
same God in others also.

. . . . .

One of the signs of the fulfilment of
the Christian Law, the will of God, is
union. . . . Our principal aim must be
to abolish all the obstacles which separate us, to hold fast only that which
unites us not only with Christians,
but also with Mohammedans, and
Buddhists, and savages. That is Christianity . . . the teaching of truth, comprehensible to all nations and all men.

. . . . .

Above all, above all—I say to you
from soul to soul; the chief aim, infinite, joyful, always attainable, and
worthy of the powers entrusted to us,
is the increase of love.

. . . . .

When an unsolved question tor-
ments one, then one feels oneself to
be a diseased member of some whole,
healthy body; one feels oneself to be
an unsound tooth in a sound body,
and one asks the whole body to help
the one member.

The whole body is God; the member is myself.

. . . . .

One should do as do the Spirit-Wrestlers—bow down to the ground before every man, remembering that in him is God. If to bow physically is impracticable, we should at all events do so spiritually.

. . . . .

The consciousness, the sensation of God who is living in me and acting through me, cannot be felt always.

There are activities to which one has got to give oneself up altogether, unlimitedly, without thinking of anything save that one thing. In these cases it is impossible to think of God; it would distract, and it is unnecessary.

One should live simply, without exertion, giving oneself up to one's tendencies; but the moment there arise inward doubt, struggle, despondency, fear, ill-will, then immediately, recognising in oneself one's spiritual being, recognising one's connection with God, one should transport oneself from the material into the spiritual region; and that not in order to escape the work of life, but, on the contrary, to gather strength for its accomplishment; for the victory over, the mastering, of the obstacle. Like a bird—to advance on one's legs with folded wings, but the moment an obstacle is encountered, then to unfold one's wings and fly up . . . and one finds relief, and one's burden disappears.

. . . . .

This is what has happened to me: I began to think more and more abstractedly about the problems of life—In what does life consist? What is its aim? What is love?—and I got farther and farther away, not only from the Old Testament conception of God the Creator, but also from the conception of Him as a Father, the righteous source of all life, and of my own being. And the Devil ensnared me, and it began to enter my mind that it is possible, and especially desirable (for union with the Chinese Confucians, with the Buddhists, and our own atheists and agnostics) altogether to avoid this conception. I thought it was possible to restrict oneself to the conception and acknowledgment of that God only which is in me, without acknowledging any God apart from that—without acknowledging the one who has implanted in me a particle of Himself. And, strange to say, I suddenly began to feel dull, depressed, and alarmed. I did not know the cause of this, but I felt that I had suddenly undergone a dreadful spiritual fall, had lost all spiritual joy and energy.

And then only did I comprehend

that this had happened because I had deserted God. And I began to think, and, strange to say, to guess whether there be a God or not; and I found Him, as it were, afresh. And I was filled with such joy, and such a firm assurance did I gain of Him, and of the possibility and duty of communion with Him, and of His hearing me, and my joy grew so great, that all these last days I have been experiencing the feeling that something very good has come to me; and I keep asking myself, "Why do I feel so happy? Yes! God! There *is* a God, and I need be neither anxious nor afraid, but can only rejoice."

I am afraid that this feeling will pass away, will grow dull; but for the present it is very joyous. It is as if I had been within a hair's-breadth of losing, nay, had thought that I had actually lost, the Being dearest to me; and yet had not so lost Him, but had only realised His priceless worth. I hope, if it does pass away, that it will only be the ecstatic feeling, but that there will remain much of what I have newly gained.

Perhaps this is what some call the "living God"; if that be so, then I did very wrongly towards them in not agreeing with but contradicting them.

The chief thing in this feeling is a

consciousness of entire security, a consciousness that He *is*, that He is good, that He knows me, and that I am entirely surrounded by Him, that I have come from Him, and am going to Him, form a part of Him, am His child. All that seems bad, seems so only because I trust to myself and not in Him, and from this life, in which it is so easy to do His will (this will at the same time being mine), I cannot fall anywhere, except only into Him ; and in Him is perfect joy and welfare.

All that I might write would not express what I have felt. Whether I am suffering physical or moral pain, whether my son be dying, or that which I love be perishing and I cannot help it, or sufferings are awaiting me— suddenly the thought recurs to me : " And how about God ? " and all becomes good and joyous and clear.

.   .   .   .   .

There is not one believing man to whom moments of doubt do not come —doubt in the existence of God. And these doubts are not harmful ; on the contrary, they lead to a higher understanding of God.

That God, whom one knew, has become familiar, and one no more believes in Him. We entirely believe in God only when He discloses Himself afresh to us. And He discloses

Himself to us from a new side when we seek Him with all our soul.

I had been thinking much about God, about the essence of my life, and, as it seemed, only to feel doubtful as to both the one and the other; and I questioned the evidence of His existence. And then, not long ago, I simply felt the desire to lean myself upon faith in God, and in the imperishableness of my soul; and to my astonishment I felt such a firm, quiet assurance as I had never felt before. So that all the doubts and testings evidently not only did not weaken, but to an enormous extent confirmed my faith.

.   .   .   .   .

One should never go to God, as it were "on purpose": "Now let me just go to God. I will begin to live according to God. I have been living according to the devil; let me now try to live according to God; who knows perhaps no harm will come of it. . . ."

There *is* harm in this, and great harm. Coming to God is something like getting married: one should do it only when one would be glad not to come to Him, or not to get married, but cannot help doing so. And therefore it is not that I would tell a man: "Go purposely into temptations"; but to him who formulates the question thus: "Well, and is it certain that I

2

will not lose by going to God instead
of to the devil?"—I would cry out as
loud as I can, "Go, go to the devil,
by all means to the devil!"

It is a hundred times better to get
well scalded against the devil than to
keep on standing at the cross roads, or
insincerely going to God.

.   .   .   .   .

I have read Herbert Spencer's reply
to Balfour;[1] the profession of Agnosticism, as they now call Atheism.

I mean, that Agnosticism, although
it wishes to be something different
from Atheism, by setting up the supposed impossibility of knowing, yet is,
in reality, the same as Atheism, because
their common root is the non-accept-
ance of a God.

.   .   .   .

And so I read Herbert Spencer, who
says, not that he *desires* to throw off
belief in God . . . but that he is
obliged to do so; self-deception is the
only other alternative. "There is no
pleasure," he says, "in the consciousness of being an infinitesimal bubble
on a globe that is itself infinitesimal
compared with the totality of things."
(I should like to ask him what he
understands by "the totality of things.")
"Those on whom the unpitying rush of

[1] From an article by Herbert Spencer on "Mr.
Balfour's Dialectics."

changes inflicts sufferings which are
often without remedy, find no consolation in the thought that they are at
the mercy of blind forces, which cause,
indifferently, now the destruction of a
sun, and now the death of an animal-
cule. Contemplation of a universe
which is without intelligible purpose
yields no satisfaction. The desire to
know what it all means is no less
strong in the Agnostic than in others,
and raises sympathy with them. Fail-
ing utterly to find any interpretation
himself, he feels a regretful inability to
accept the interpretations they offer."

Someone else was saying exactly
the same thing to me the other day,
" A sort of circum-rotation takes place,
and in the centre of this vortex, end-
less in time and place, *I* appear, live,
and disappear. This is certain. All
the rest—*i.e.* the conception of some
intelligent being, from which I have
proceeded, and for the attainment of
whose object I exist in common with
all that exists—such a conception is a
self-deception."

There are two distinct and mutually
contradictory theories of the universe
which may be represented thus—

The Agnostic says, " I observe myself, a being born of my parents, in the
same way as I observe all other living
beings which surround me, and which

exist under certain conditions subject
to my examination and study; and I
study myself and other objects, both
animate and inanimate, and the conditions in which they exist. And in
accordance with this study I order my
life. Questions as to origin I investi-
gate in the same way, both by observation and by experiment, and I attain a
greater and greater knowledge of them.
As to the question whence all this
universe has proceeded, why it exists,
and why I exist in it, I leave it unanswered, as I do not see the possibility
of answering it as definitely, clearly,
and convincingly as I answer questions
concerning the conditions of things *in*
the universe. And therefore the answer
to this question which consists in saying that there exists a supposed
rational Being, a God, from whom I
have proceeded (it is generally said,
'from whom the world proceeds,' by
which is meant the creation of the
world, which the Christian teaching
does not affirm), which Being, for
some reason known to itself, has
determined the law of my life—this
answer to the question I do not accept,
as it does not contain the clearness
and demonstrability possessed by the
scientific answers to the questions concerning the causes and conditions of
various natural phenomena."

So says the Agnostic, and in not admitting the possibility of any other knowledge but what is acquired by observation and the analysis of observation, he is, if not right, at least quite logical and consistent.

The Christian, on the other hand, acknowledging God, says, "I am conscious that I exist only because I feel myself to be a rational being. And in feeling myself to be so, I cannot but recognise that my life and that of all that exists must be equally rational. And in order to be so it must have an object. The object of my life must be outside myself, in that Being for which both I and all that exist serve as instruments for the attainment of the object of life. This Being does exist, and I must, in my life, fulfil its law or will. Questions as to the nature of this Being which demands of me the fulfilment of its law, and as to when and how, in time and space, this rational life originated in me, and originates in other beings — that is, 'What is God?' 'Is He personal or impersonal?' 'Did He create the world, and how?' 'When did a soul awake in me?' 'At what time, and how did it originate in others?' 'Whence has it come and whither will it go?' 'In what part of the body does it reside?'—all these questions I must leave unanswered, because I know beforehand that in the region of their observation and analysis I shall never come to a definite answer, as all will disappear into the infinitude of time and space. It is for this reason that I do not accept the answers given by science as to how the universe (the suns and worlds) has originated, how the soul originates, and in what part of the brain it is located."

In the first instance, the Agnostic, acknowledging himself to be a mere animal, and therefore admitting that he is subject only to external sensations, does not admit a spiritual origin, and resigns himself to that senselessness of existence which violates the demands of reason.

In the second instance, the Christian, acknowledging himself to be only a rational being, and therefore accepting only that which corresponds to the demands of reason, does not acknowledge the adequacy of the data of external experience, and considers those data fantastic and erroneous.

Both are equally right. But the difference between them, and an essential one, lies in the fact that, according to the former conception, everything in the universe is strictly scientific, logical, and rational, except the meaning of the life itself of man and the whole universe. And they have no meaning. And consequently, from such a conception, there may proceed very many interesting and amusing considerations ; but, notwithstanding all efforts to the contrary, nothing necessary for guidance in life. Whereas, according to the latter conception, the life of man and of the whole universe acquires a definite, rational meaning, which has the most direct, simple, and universally accessible adaptability to life, at the same time not excluding the possibility of scientific investigations ; which, in this case, are put in their proper place.

To - day, science investigates the universe "behind time," from the pagan standpoint ; endeavouring to conquer it by power for man's personal or social welfare ; whereas the religion of our day has for long been demanding another relation : the study of the universe from the standpoint of personal subjugation to the higher Will. And it is this science, in its object two thousand years behind time, which wishes to determine the basis of morality !

One of the superstitions that most confuse our metaphysical conceptions is the superstition that the world was created, that it arose out of nothing, and that there is a God-Creator.

In reality we have no ground for imagining a God-Creator, nor any necessity. The Chinese and Indians have no such conception, and moreover a Creator, a Providence, is incompatible with the Christian God-Father, God-Spirit. The God who is Love, a particle of whom lives in me, constitutes my life; and the manifestation and avocation of this particle constitutes the meaning of my life.

God the Creator is indifferent, and allows suffering and evil. God the Spirit delivers from suffering and evil, and is always perfect welfare. A God-Creator there is not. There is *myself* acknowledging the universe through the faculties given me; and inwardly recognising my Father-God. He is the origin of my spiritual self—the external world is only my limit.

.   .   .   .   .

People often speak of the evil which God causes to men (for instance when they are overcome with grief at the loss of one they love), and while so saying and thinking, they imagine that they believe in God, and they pray to Him.

God does evil! And, if God does evil, He is not good, not Love; and, if He is not good, then He does not exist.

This comes of people being so certain that what they do wrongly is not only good but excellent—as when they affirm that to give all one's love to one's children is very good. Then, when they experience the evil which is only the result of their own mistakes, their own sins, they blame, not themselves, but God. And therefore, in the depth of their soul, they acknowledge God to be evil, that is, deny Him, and therefore do not receive consolation from Him.

.   .   .   .   .

It is into God one must penetrate. There only can one unite with others.

.   .   .   .   .

The moral law, being founded on phenomena of life, will always be local, temporary, casual, and, above all, doubtful. Whatsoever general reasons may be put forward, why I should act thus and not otherwise in this indefinite universe, I will always find, or will feel, the existence of other yet more general reasons which will overthrow the demands put before me; and so on to infinity.

And therefore no temporary law, not founded upon the relation to the infinite, can ever be certain. Only such a relation to the universe, or to the mind of the universe, to God, from which flows a certain continual direction of conduct, can be the basis of morality. And so has it always been, and so it is.

.   .   .   .   .

Nothing better proves the existence of God than the attempts of the evolutionists to accept morality and deduce it from the struggle for existence. It is obvious that morality cannot emanate from struggle; and yet they feel that we cannot do without it, acknowledge its existence, and endeavour to deduce it from their own propositions; though to deduce it from the theory of evolution is as strange (or even more so) and illogical as to deduce it from the ordinances given by the Hebrew God on Sinai. Their mistake, which consists in denying the consciousness of one's spiritual self as a product of God, a particle of Him, without which there can be no rational view of life,—this mistake forces them to admit an unjustifiable and even contradictory mystery: to admit in the form of morality that same God whom they have excluded from their view of life.

The other day a Frenchman asked me, "Would it not be sufficient to base morality upon righteousness and beauty?"—again that same God whom they are afraid to name.

.   .   .   .   .

Let us endeavour to express that which we know, that which is necessary to us, joyful and certain; and God (the same whom you think it necessary to evade) will help us. By naming Him I acknowledge my incompleteness; I, His weak, small vessel, endeavour to open myself—that part of me which can receive Him—in order that He may enter into me in so far as I am able and worthy to receive Him.

Above all, He is necessary to me in order that I may express whither I am tending and to whom I go. In this monotonous earthly life I may not feel Him, I may do without this form of thought and expression; but in relation to the passage from the past life into this one, and from this one into another, I cannot avoid expressing by Him that from whence I come and whither I am going, this being the form of expression nearest to the true character of the case; from God to God,—from that which is outside of time and space to the same again.

.   .   .   .   .

The will of God is known to every man much more than the will of society, of the State. Man is not, as those on the lowest plane of understanding think, an individual or social animal only; but man is a particle of the Divine, contained in a bodily shell.

Man is the son of God, and knows his
Father, and his Will. To do the will of
the Father, one must know Him, be conscious of Him ; and the man who knows
the Father always knows His will.

Ignorance of His will is produced
not by the impossibility of knowing it,
but by the non-fulfilment of the two
first requirements of Christ ; from the
non-acknowledgment of the insig-
nificance of the personal life ; and
from not denying it.

.   .   .   .   .

It is not that I altogether agree
with what you say about the understanding and about God, but my
thoughts are not in conformity with
yours. I do not say that I agree, because in speaking about these matters
it is often difficult to express accurately
what one thinks, and words may say
too much or too little, and therefore it
is never possible to admit that a certain
way of formulating completely corresponds to one's conception. But I see
that we think and feel in the same
direction, and this gives me great
pleasure. It is impossible not to think
about these matters, but each of us
involuntarily thinks in his own way.
To formulate one's thoughts, in the
way it has been done in various creeds,
is not only useless, but may be dangerous. It is possible and necessary to

formulate deductions which are applic-
able to life, as did Moses: "Thou shalt
not kill!" or Christ: "Resist not evil!"
I repeat, however, that I think in the
same direction, and quite agree with
you that the understanding is attainable
in proportion to one's purity, humility,
and love.

Striving towards God, towards the
purity of the Divine Essence in me,
towards that life for which this is here
purified, I indirectly, somehow, attain
more surely and more exactly both
the general and my own welfare, without hurry, without doubt, and with
joy.
And help me, God!

Father, help me to fulfil Thy law
in all humility, purity, and love, and
to find therein a perpetual source of
joy.

Lord, take me, teach me, enter into
me. Be one with me, or destroy me.
Without Thee I will not, I cannot
live. There is no life without Thee,
Father.

I like to address God. If there were
no God, the call into empty space were
in itself good. From such an appeal,
all those weaknesses of vanity, self-

complacency, self-interest, from which
it is hardly possible to be free when
appealing to men, are absent.

So help me, Father!

.   .   .   .   .

To be ready to pass for a fool, a
deceiver; to know that in any case one
will so pass. To dirty one's hands in
order not to be afraid of grasping dirty
things. And then to live not for
reputation in the world! It is easy
to say all this, but when one has been
used to live for reputation, and wishes
to give it up, there is nothing to
live for except God. It is "a vicious
circle." If one lives to God, one will
disregard the opinion of men. If one
disregard the opinion of men, one will
learn to live for God; there is nothing
else to live for.

.   .   .   .   .

No living man will ever fulfil the
will of God perfectly. But because
we see and know the impossibility of
complete fulfilment, it does not follow
that we should determine beforehand
to fulfil it incompletely, partially—
(this is a most common, dreadful sin).
But we should, on the contrary, incessantly and always strive for its
complete fulfilment. "Seek ye first
the kingdom of God."

.   .   .   .   .

The desire for good is not God, but

only one of His manifestations; one of the sides from which we see God. God manifests Himself in me by the desire for good.

. . . . .

The God contained in man at first seeks to free Himself by expanding, enlarging the being in whom He is contained; then, realising the unsurmountable limitations of that being, He seeks to free Himself by emerging from it and enveloping other beings.

. . . . .

The rational being is not containable by the life of the individual, but the moment it becomes rational seeks to emerge from that life.

The Christian teaching shows to man that the essence of his life is not his separate being but God, contained in this being. And God is recognised in man through reason and love.

Above all, the desire for personal welfare, self-love, exists in man only while reason has not awakened in him. As soon as reason has awakened, it becomes clear to man that the desire for the welfare of himself, his separate being, is fruitless; because welfare is unrealisable for the separate inert being. As soon as reason appears the desire for only one kind of welfare becomes ·possible—universal welfare;

for in universal welfare there is no
strife but union; no death but the
transmission of life. God is not love
itself, but in unrational beings He
manifests Himself in self-love; in
rational beings in universal love.

. . . . .

Nature, it is said, is economical with
her forces—with the least effort she
attains the greatest effects. So also
with God. To establish on earth the
kingdom of God, unity, mutual service,
and to destroy enmity, God does not
need to accomplish it Himself. He
has implanted in Man his reason, which
liberates love, and all that He desires
will be done by man. God does His
work through us. Time does not exist
for Him, or exists only in eternity.
Having implanted in man rational love,
God has done all.

Why has He done it thus, through
man, and not through Himself? The
question is futile, and would never
have suggested itself were we not all
perverted by the absurd superstition
of the "creation" of the world by
God.

. . . . .

What follows when man recognises
as his real Ego not his separate being,
but God, who is living in him? Firstly,
such a man, not consciously desiring
his own personal welfare, either will

not at all or at least will not so strenu-
ously deprive others of it. Secondly,
having acknowledged as his Ego, God,
who desires universal welfare, man
must desire the same.

. . . .

Prayer is addressed to a personal
God, not because He is a person (I
even know with certainty that He is
not a person, because personality is
limitation, and God is unlimited), but
because I am a personal being. I have
a piece of green glass before my eyes,
and therefore everything appears green
to me: it cannot appear otherwise,
although I know it is not green.

. . . .

Riding home from Toula I was
thinking "I am a part of Him, in a
certain way, separated from other such
parts. He is the All — the Father."
And I experienced the feeling of love
towards Him. Now, especially just at
the present moment, I am unable not
only to revive, but even to recall this
feeling. And yet it was so joyful that
I said to myself, "Well, I thought I
should no more experience any new
feeling, and now I have learnt a
wonderful, blissful new feeling." Yes,
feeling, that is the word.

. . . .

It is said that God should be con-
ceived as a personality. This is a

great misunderstanding; personality is limitation. Man feels himself a personality only because he is in contact with other personalities. If he were alone, he would not be a person. These two conceptions—the external world (other beings), and our own personality, mutually define one another. If there were not the world of other beings, man would not be conscious of his own personality, nor realise the possibility of the existence of other beings. And therefore a man, in the world, cannot conceive himself otherwise than as a person.

But how can we say of God that He is a person? Herein lies the root of anthropomorphism. We can only say of God that which Mahomet and Moses said: that "He is One." But there can be no notion of number in relation to God, therefore this implies not that He is one numerically, but that He is one—centred: not a conception, but a being—that which the orthodox call "the living God" in contrast to the pantheistic God; that is, the highest spiritual being who lives in all. He *is* one in the sense that He exists as a being who can be addressed; that is, that there is a relation between me, a limited personality, and God, unfathomable but existing.

We know God as a single being, we

cannot know Him otherwise, and yet we cannot realise one single being as pervading all. In this we find the chief incomprehensibleness of God. If God be not One, then He becomes diffused, non-existent, whereas if He be One, then we involuntarily represent Him to ourselves as a personality, and He is no longer the Higher Being, the All. And, nevertheless, to know God, to lean on Him, we are forced to conceive Him both as pervading all, and at the same time as One.

. . . . .

The world is certainly not such as we conceive it. Other instruments of perception will give us other worlds. But however that which we call the world may change, our relation to it is undoubtedly as we conceive it, is unchangeable, being based on that in us which perceives; and which perceives not only in me but in all conscious life. This perceiving element is the same everywhere, in all, and in oneself. It is both God Himself, and that limited part of Him which constitutes my real self.

But what is this God,—the eternal, infinite, omnipotent, which has become mortal, limited, weak? Wherefore has God subdivided Himself? I do not know, but I do know that this is so, and that in this is life. All that we

know is nought else than a similar subdivision of God. All which we cognise
as the world is but the perception of
these divisions. Our perception of the
world, that which we call matter in
time and space, is the contact of the
limits of our Divinity and the other
subdivisions of God. Birth and death
are transitions from one subdivision
to another.

.   .   .   .   .

The strictest and most consistent
Agnostic recognises God whether he
wishes to or not. He cannot but
recognise that his existence and the
existence of the whole world has some
sense, inaccessible to him, and that there
is a law of his life, a law to which
he can submit, and from which he can
deviate. It is just this recognition of
a higher sense of life, inaccessible to
man, but necessarily existing, and of
the law of one's life, which is the recognition of God and His will.

And such a recognition of God is
much firmer than the belief in God
as Creator, Trinity, Redeemer, Ruler,
etc.

To believe so is to have dug through
the rubble to the solid rock, and to
have built the house thereon.

.   .   .   .   .

Men know two Gods: one whom
they wish to compel to serve them,

demanding from Him in prayers the fulfilment of *their* desires; and another God, whom it is for us to serve, and to the fulfilment of whose will all our efforts should be directed.

.   .   .   .   .

Just now, having found myself alone after my work, I asked myself what I should do next, and being free from any personal desires (except the physical demands which are felt when one desires food or sleep), I felt most vividly the joy of the consciousness of the will of God, of requiring and desiring nothing but to fulfil that which He wishes.

This feeling was evoked by the question which I put to myself in solitude and quiet, "Who am I? What am I?" And the answer came of itself so clearly, "Whoever and whatever thou art, thou art sent by someone, to do something. Well, then, do it!" And so joyously, so well, did I feel my fusion with the will of God.

.   .   .   .   .

What am I here, abandoned in the midst of this world? To whom shall I turn? From whom shall I seek an answer?—From men?

They do not know; they laugh; they do not wish to know. They say, "That is nonsense. Do not think about it. Here is the world and its attractions—live!"

But they shall not deceive me. I know that they do not believe what they say. They too, like me, are tormented, and suffer from the fear of death, of themselves, and of Thee, Lord, whom they do not wish to name.

I too, for long did not name Thee, and I too did the same that they do. I know this deception, and how it oppresses the heart, and how terrible is the fire of despair which is concealed in the heart of him who does not name Thee. However much they strive to quench it, it will burn up their heart as it used to burn mine.

But, Lord, I named Thee, and my sufferings ceased. My despair has passed.

I hate my weakness, I seek Thy way, but I do not despair. I feel Thy nearness, feel Thy help when I walk in Thy ways, and Thy pardon when I stray from them.

Thy way is clear and plain. Thy yoke easy and Thy burden light, but I have long wandered outside Thy ways, long in the abominations of my youth have I proudly flung off every burden, freed myself from every yoke, and untaught myself to walk in Thy ways; and both Thy yoke and Thy burden

have become heavy for me, though I
know they are good and light.

Lord, pardon the errors of my youth,
and help me to bear Thy yoke as joy-
fully as I accept it.

PRINTED BY
MORRISON AND GIBB LIMITED
EDINBURGH

THREEPENCE

By Leo
Tolstoy

Free Age Press
1900

The Free Age Press stands for an attempt to assist in spreading those deep convictions in which the noblest spirits of every age and race have united—that man's true aim and happiness is "unity in reason and love"; the realisation of the brotherhood of all men,—and that we *must* all strive to purge away, each from himself, those false ideas, false feelings, and false desires, personal, social, religious, political, racial, economic, which alienate us one from another and produce nine-tenths of the sum of human suffering.

Of these truly Christian and universally religious aspirations the writings of Leo Tolstoy are perhaps to-day the most definite expression, and it is to the production of 1d., 3d., and 6d. editions of all his known religious, social, and ethical works, together with the unpublished matter and future writings to which we have and shall have special access (being in close relationship with Tolstoy) that *The Free Age Press* will at first devote itself, trusting that all who sympathise will assist by every means in their power, especially in helping to spread the books the world over, losing no opportunity of introducing them whenever and wherever feasible, and of so making it possible for the work to be continued, and extended into wider and wider fields. As it is Tolstoy's desire that his books shall not be copyrighted, our editions will, whenever possible, be free to the world.

Suggestions, criticisms, inquiries, offers of help, and co-operation will be gratefully welcomed and it is specially requested that the names of any books that have helped towards a better understanding of life may be furnished, so that a much needed list may be compiled and published.

Letters, Private Orders, and Money Orders (it is hoped that friends will *purchase* as many copies as possible: even one will help) should be addressed to THE EDITORS, "FREE AGE PRESS," MALDON, ESSEX. *Booksellers* must order of Messrs. SIMPKIN, MARSHALL, HAMILTON, KENT & CO. LTD., London, E.C.; THE CLARION CO. LTD., 72 Fleet Street, E.C.; Messrs. JOHN MENZIES & CO., Glasgow; and Mr. HEYWOOD, Manchester.

RELIGION
AND . . .
MORALITY

By LEO .
TOLSTOY

THE FREE AGE PRESS
CHRISTCHURCH, HANTS . .
(New Address)

1900

RELIGION AND MORALITY[1]

———◆———

You ask me—first, How I understand the word *religion*; and, second, Whether I admit the existence of morality, independent of religion as understood by me. I will answer these most important questions, well put by you, as best I can.

There are three separate meanings generally implied by the word *religion*. First—That religion is a certain true revelation given by God to men, from which proceeds man's worship of God. Such an interpretation is applied to religion by all believers in one of its existing forms, who regard in consequence their particular form as the only true one. Second—That religion is a collection of superstitious statements, from which a worship equally superstitious is derived. Such an interpretation is applied to religion by sceptics in general; by those, that is, who do not believe in the religion they are defining. Third—That religion is a compilation of propositions and rules, invented by clever men, and a necessity for

[1] A reply to two questions put by the German Ethical Society. First printed in *Contemporary Review*, 1894. Revised and corrected.

the vulgar herd, as much for their consolation as for their subjugation and the
restraint of their passions. Such an interpretation is applied to religion by those
indifferent to it personally, but who regard
it as a useful instrument in the governance
of mankind.

By the first definition, religion is an
indubitable and irrefragable truth, the pro-
pagation of which amongst all men and by
every possible means is necessary to the
welfare of mankind. By the second, religion is a mass of superstition from which
it is desirable, and even needful to the
welfare of humanity, that mankind should
be delivered. By the third, religion is a
contrivance useful to humanity, though unnecessary for those of the highest development, but which, as indispensable to the
consolation and control of the vulgar, it is
needful to maintain.

The first definition is similar to one a
man might make of music, by defining it
as his most familiar and favourite song,
with which it is desirable that the greatest
number of people possible should be acquainted. The second, in the same connection, would be that applied to music by
a man who, not understanding it, therefore
not caring for it, called it the production
of sound by the throat, mouth, or hands
upon certain instruments; a useless and
even objectionable occupation, from which
it was necessary to wean men as soon as
possible. The third is similar to that
which a man would apply to music, who

considered it a useful contrivance for teaching men to dance or to march, for which
purposes it should be maintained.

The difference and narrowness of these
definitions arise from their failure to
take hold of the *essence* of music, merely
defining its features from the definer's
point of view. So is it also with the three
definitions of religion. According to the
first, religion is whatever the definer thinks
that he is right in believing. According
to the second, it is that which, in the
definer's opinion, people are wrong in believing. According to the third, it is, by
the standard of the definer, what it is
beneficial to make men believe. All which
define, not what constitutes the essence of
religion, but the definer's belief of what
religion constitutes. The first supplants
the notion of religion, by the faith of him
who defines; the second, by the faith by
which other people regard it; the third,
by the faith of men in whatever may be
supplied them as religion.

But what is faith? Why do people
believe in what they believe? What is
faith? and whence has it arisen?

Amongst the majority of the educated
classes it is regarded as a settled question
that the essence of every religion has its
origin in the personification, deification,
and worship of the forces of Nature—proceeding from superstitious fear of Nature's
incomprehensible phenomena. This view
is accepted, without criticism, by the
educated crowd of our time, and it not

only does not meet with any refutation
from men of science, but, for the most
part, finds, precisely among them, most
definite confirmation. If, indeed, voices
are at times heard, as that of Max Müller
and others, which attribute to religion
another origin and sense, these voices are
unheard and unnoticed in the general and
almost unanimous affirmation that religion
is the outcome of ignorance and superstition.

Not long ago, at the beginning of the
nineteenth century, if the most advanced
thinkers rejected Catholicism, Protestant-
ism, and Greek orthodoxy, as did the
Encyclopedists at the end of the eighteenth,
still not one of them denied that religion
in general has been and is an indispensable
condition in the lives of all. Not to mention the Deists—as Bernardin de St. Pierre,
Diderot, and Rousseau—Voltaire raised a
monument to God, and Robespierre proclaimed a festal day in honour of the
Supreme Being. But at the present day,
thanks to the frivolous and superficial
teaching of Auguste Comte (who sincerely
believed, in common with the majority of
Frenchmen, that Christianity is nothing
but Catholicism, and therefore saw in
Catholicism the complete realisation of
Christianity); the educated crowd, which
always readily and greedily accepts the
lowest view, have decided and acknowledged that religion is only a certain long-
obsolete aspect in the development of
humanity which hinders progress. It is

agreed that humanity has already outlived
two periods, the religious and metaphysical,
and has now entered into the third and
highest, the scientific, and that all religious
phenomena are only the survivals of an
outgrown spiritual organ of humanity, once
needful, but long ago lost to sense and
significance.

It is agreed that religion had its origin
in the worship of imaginary beings, evoked
by fear of the incomprehensible forces of
Nature, as in ancient times Democritus
thought, and as affirmed by the philosophers and historians of religion. But,
putting aside the fact that the recognition
of some unseen and supernatural being or
beings has not always proceeded from a
sense of fear evoked by unknown forces
of Nature, as is proved by hundreds
of advanced and learned thinkers of the
past—Socrates, Descartes, Newton—and
like men of our own times, who, being in
no wise fearful of such forces, admitted
the existence of some supreme supernatural
being or beings—the affirmation that religion has been the outcome of man's superstitious fear of the incomprehensible powers
of Nature, in reality does not answer the
chief question, From what in man does
the idea of an unseen and supernatural
being derive existence? If men were
afraid of thunder and lightning, they
would fear them as thunder and lightning;
but why invent an unseen and supernatural
Jove, living in certain regions, and occasion-
ally flinging bolts at men? If men were

astounded by the aspect of death, they would fear to die; but why invent souls of the dead with whom to enter into imaginary communion? From thunder men might hide; from the fear of death they might fly; but instead they devised an eternal, all-powerful Being, on whom they reckon themselves dependent, and the living souls of the dead—not from fear alone, but for some other reasons. And in these reasons, evidently, lies the essence of what is called religion.

Moreover, every man who has ever felt the religious sentiment, if only in childhood, knows from his own experience that such a sentiment has always been awakened in him, not by external, terrifying, material phenomena, but by an internal consciousness of his own frailty, solitude, and sinfulness, and connected not at all with any dread of the unknown forces of Nature. Hence man may, both by external observation and by personal experience, ascertain that religion is not the worship of deities, evoked by superstitious fear of unknown natural forces, and only proper to mankind at a certain period of their development, but something independent altogether of fear, or of a degree of culture, and not liable to destruction by any access of enlightenment; just as man's consciousness of his finality in the infinite universe, and of his sinfulnesss (*i.e.* his non-fulfilment of all he might and ought to have done), always has existed and always will exist while man remains man.

In truth, every man, as soon as he
emerges from the animal existence of
infancy and childhood—during which he
lives by the pressure of those claims which
are presented to him by his animal nature
—every man who is awake to reasonable
consciousness cannot fail to remark how
the life about him renews itself, unde-
stroyed, and steadfastly subordinate to
one definite eternal law ; and that he alone,
self-recognised as a creature separate from
the entire universe, is condemned to death,
to a disappearance in unbounded space and
limitless time, and to the painful consciousness of responsibility for his actions—a
consciousness, so to say, that, having acted
not well, he might have acted better.
And, with this understanding, every
reasoning man must stop, think, and ask
himself—wherefore this momentary, indefinite, unstable existence within a universe uncompassed, eternal, firmly defined ?
Man cannot, when he enters into his
full measure of life, elude this question.
It confronts all, and all in some fashion
answer it, and it is this answer which is
the essence of religion ; the answer to the
question, Wherefore do I live, and what is
my relation to the infinite universe about
me ? All religious metaphysics — their
teaching as to deities, the origin of existence,
external worship—though generally taken
for religion, are only the various signs
accompanying religion, and changing with
a change in its geographical, historical, or
ethnographical conditions.   There is no

religion, however cultured, however crude, but has its beginnings in the assessment of the relations of man to the surrounding universe or to its first cause. There is no ceremony of religion so rustic, nor ritual so refined, which has not a like foundation. All the teaching of religion is the expression of the relations in which the founder of the religion regards himself— and therefore all mankind—as standing towards the universe or towards its origin and first cause.

The expressions of these relations are very numerous, and correspond to the conditions of race and time in which the founder of the religion and those appropriating it are placed. Moreover, these expressions are variously misinterpreted and deformed by the founder's disciples, who, often for hundreds, sometimes for thousands of years, are in advance of the understanding of the masses. Hence many accounts appear to exist of this relation of man to the universe, called religions ; but in substance there are only three relations to the universe or its first cause of an essential quality : (1) The primitive personal relation ; (2) the pagan social, or family, or State relation ; (3) the Christian or godly relation. Strictly speaking, man can only be related to the universe in two ways : the *personal*, which is the recognition of life as the welfare of the individual, separately or in union with others ; and the *Christian*, which is the recognition of life as the service of Him who sent man into the world. The social relation of man to the universe is merely an enlargement of the personal.

The first 'of these recognitions (or perceptions), which is the most ancient, and which is now found only amongst men of the lowest order of development, consists in the consideration by man of himself as a self-sufficient being, existing with the sole purpose of obtaining for himself the greatest possible amount of personal happiness from the world about him, indifferent to the amount of suffering thus entailed on other creatures. From this early conception of a relation to the universe—which suffices for every child, as it sufficed for humanity on the threshold of its development, and still satisfies many savage tribes and men of a coarse moral fibre—have proceeded all the ancient heathen religions, as well as the corrupt and lower forms of more recent religions, as Buddhism,[1] Taoism, Mohammedanism, and Christianity in its perverted issues. To this same perception the more modern spiritism owes its origin, being founded on the preservation and welfare of the

[1] Buddhism, although it demands from its disciples resignation of all the pleasures of the world, and even of life itself, is founded on the same idea of an individual sufficient for himself, and predestined to happiness, or rather—in comparison with the right of man to enjoyment as proclaimed by positive heathenism—to the absence of pain. Heathenism holds that the universe should serve the interest of the individual, Buddhism that the universe must be dissolved as the producing factor in the miseries of mankind. Buddhism is only negative heathenism.

individual. All heathen superstitions, divination, deification of beings in blissful existence with the attributes of men, or of saints interceding for men, all sacrifices and supplications for earthly advantages or protection from calamity, proceed from the same conception of life.

The second or social pagan conception of man's relation to the universe, established in the next stage of development and natural to the state of manhood, consists in the admission that the meaning of life is to be discovered, not in the happiness of individuals, but in the welfare of a certain association of them, as the family, tribe, State, nation, even humanity (according to the attempted religion of the Positivists). In this perception, the attention is transferred from the individual to the family, tribe, State, or nation—that is, to an association of individuals, the welfare of whom is, in this case, regarded as the object of existence. All patriarchal and social religions of a like character have their origin in this conception : the religions of the Chinese, Japanese, of the chosen people of the Jews, the State religion of the Romans, our own religion of Church and State, debased to this connection by Augustine, and wrongly called Christian, and the Positivists' hypothetical religion of "humanity." Ancestor-worship in China and Japan, emperor-worship in Rome, the manifold ceremonies of the Jews to preserve their covenant with God, all family, social, Church, Christian

Te Deums for the welfare of the State, and for military success, are founded on this same conception of the relation of man to the universe.

The third conception of this relation—the Christian one—of which every man of advanced years is involuntarily conscious, and upon which humanity, in my opinion, is now entering, consists in the acknowledgment by man that the meaning of life is not to be found in the attainment of his own individual aim, nor in the attainment of that of any association of individuals, but solely in serving that Supreme Will, which has produced man and the entire universe, for the attainment, not of the aims of man, but of the Superior Will which has produced him. From this conception, the loftiest religious teaching known to us has proceeded, germs of which existed in the teaching of the Pythagoreans, Therapeutics, Essenes, Egyptians, Persians, Brahmins, Buddhists, and Taoists, in their best representatives, but which has only received its final and fullest expression in the true, unperverted interpretation of Christianity. All the ritual of those ancient religions proceeding from this conception of life, all the modern external forms of association of the Unitarians, Universalists, Quakers, Nazarenes, and Russian Spirit - Wrestlers (Doukhobors),[1]

---

[1] A section of the so-called sectarians, having a spiritual conception of life and the Gospels, and who claim to fight against the flesh by the aid of the Spirit.

and all so-called rationalistic sects, their
sermons, hymns, intercourse, and books,
are religious manifestations of this conception of man's relation to the universe.

All possible religions of every kind are
inevitably distributed between these three
conceptions. Every man who has emerged
from the animal condition must invariably
adopt one of these conceptions of his
relation to the universe, and in this
adoption consists the real religion of every
man, outside any confession of faith to
which he may nominally adhere. Every
man inevitably, one way or another,
pictures to himself his own relation to
the universe, because a rational being
cannot live in the world without some
sort of consciousness of his relation to it.
And as only three explanations of this
relation have been produced by humanity,
and are known to us, every man must
inevitably hold by one of the three, and,
whether he will or not, belongs to one of
the three fundamental religions, among
which all humanity may be divided. And
hence the general assertion made by men
of culture in the Christian world that they
have reached the summit of development,
where they neither have nor need a
religion, only means that, renouncing
Christianity, the one religion proper to
our time, they hold with one of the lower
religions—either with the social-family-
State religion, or with that of primitive
heathendom—without being aware of the
tendency themselves. A man without a

religion—that is, without any perceptive
relation to the universe—is as impossible
as a man without a heart. He may be as
unaware of the possession of one as of the
other, but neither without a heart nor
without a religion can man exist. Religion is the relation which man acknowledges towards the universe about him, or
to its source and first cause, and a rational
man must perforce be in some sort of
perceptive relationship.

But you may perhaps say that the
definition of man's relation to the universe
is a subject not for religion, but for
philosophy, or, in general, for science,
allowing that the latter term includes
philosophy. I do not think so. I hold,
on the contrary, that the supposition that
science in its widest sense, including
philosophy, should define the relation of
man to the universe is altogether erroneous,
and the chief source of disorder in the
ideas of our educated society as to religion,
science, and morality. Science, including
philosophy, cannot define the relation of
mankind to the infinite universe or to its
source; if only because, before any sort
of science or of philosophy could have
been formulated, a conception of some sort
of relationship of man to the universe,
without which no kind of mental activity
is possible, must have existed. As a man
cannot by any kind of movement discover
the direction in which he must move, yet
all movement is made inevitably in some
given direction, so it is impossible, by the

mental efforts of philosophy or of science,
to discover the direction in which this
effort should be made, but every mental
effort is inevitably accomplished in some
direction which has been given it already.
And this direction for all mental effort is
always indicated by religion. All philo-
sophies known to us, from Plato to
Schopenhauer, have followed inevitably
the direction given by religion.

The philosophy of Plato and of his
followers was a pagan system to procure
the maximum of happiness, as well for
the individual as for the association of
individuals in the form of a State. The
Church-Christian philosophy of the Middle
Ages, based on the same pagan conception
of existence, investigated means of salvation for the individual—that is, the means
for procuring his best advantage in a future
life—and only in its theocratic endeavours
did it touch on the welfare of societies.
The modern philosophy of Hegel, as well
as that of Comte, is founded on the State-
social-religious conception of existence.
The pessimistic philosophy of Schopenhauer and Hartmann, which desired to
free itself from the Jewish religious conception, became unwittingly subject to the
basis of Buddhism. Philosophy always
has been and always will be merely the
investigation of the *results* of the relation
of man to the universe inculcated by
religion, for until this conception is
acquired there is no material for philosophical investigation.

It is just the same with positive science in the strict meaning of the term. Such a science always has been, and always will be, merely the investigation of such objects and phenomena as appear to demand inquiry in consequence of a certain conception of the relation of man to the universe instituted by religion. Science always has been, and always will be, not the study of "everything," as men of science at present naively imagine (a thing which is, moreover, impossible, as the subjects in the scope of study are innumerable), but only of those things which, in order and according to their degree of importance, religion selects from the infinite objects, phenomena, and circumstances, into which inquiry may be made.

And hence there is not one science, but as many sciences as there are religions. Each religion selects a certain circle of subjects which must be studied, and hence the science of every time and nation inevitably bears the character of its religion in the point of view from which its examination is made. So the pagan science, reinstituted at the Renaissance, and flourishing at present among us under the title of Christian, always has been, and continues to be, merely an investigation of the circumstances by which man may attain the highest welfare, and of those phenomena of the universe which may be put under contribution to the same end. The philosophical science of Brahmin and

Buddhist has always been merely the investigation of circumstances by which man may be delivered from the miseries which oppress him. The Jewish science (of the Talmud) has always been the study and explanation of those conditions which must be observed by man in order to ratify his covenant with God, and to preserve the chosen nation at the highest level of its election. The Church-Christian science was and is the investigation of those circumstances by which man procures his salvation. The true Christian science, that which is but just at the birth, is the investigation of those circumstances by which man may become acquainted with the demands of the Supreme Will, whose instrument he is, and how he may fit them to his existence.

Neither philosophy nor science can institute the relation of man to the universe, because such reciprocity must have existence before any kind of science or philosophy can begin; since each investigates phenomena by means of the intellect, and independent of the position or sensations of the investigator; whereas the relation of man to the universe is defined, not by the intellect alone, but by his sensitive perception, aided by all his spiritual powers. However much one may assure and instruct a man that all real existence is an idea only, that matter is made up of atoms, that the essence of life is corporality or will, that heat, light, movement, electricity are different mani-

festations of one and the same energy, one
cannot thereby explain to a being with
pains, pleasures, fears, and hopes, his
position in the universe. That position,
and his consequent relation to the universe,
is explained only by religion, which says,
"The universe exists for thee, and therefore take from life all that thou canst
obtain;" or else, "Thou art one of the
favourite people of God; serve that people,
and accomplish the instructions of that
God, and thou and thy people shall be
partakers of the highest bliss;" or else,
"Thou art the instrument of a Supreme
Will, which has sent thee into the universe
to accomplish a work predestined for thee;
learn that will, and do it, and thou wilt
do for thyself the best that thou canst
do."

To understand philosophy and science,
one needs study and preparation, but
neither is required for the understanding
of religion: that is at once comprehensible
to every man, whatever his ignorance and
limitations. A man need acquire neither
philosophy nor science to understand his
relation to the universe, or to its source;
a superfluity of knowledge, encumbering
his consciousness, is rather an impediment;
but he must renounce, if only for the
time, the vanity of the world, and acquire
a sense of his material frailty and of truth,
which are, as the Gospels tell us, to be
found most often in children and in the
simplest, most unlearned, of men. For
this reason we see the most simple,

ignorant and untaught men accept clearly,
consciously, and easily the highest Christian
conception of life, whereas the most learned
and cultured linger in crude paganism.
As, for example, we observe men of refine-
ment and education whose conception of
existence is the acquirement of personal
pleasure or security from pain, as with the
shrewd and cultured Schopenhauer, or in
the salvation of the soul by sacraments
and means of grace, as with learned
bishops of the Church; whereas an almost
illiterate sectarian peasant in Russia, without the slightest mental effort, achieves
the same conception of life as was accomplished by the greatest sages of the world
—Epictetus, Marcus Aurelius, Seneca—
namely, the consciousness of one's being
as the instrument of the will of God—the
son of God.

But you may ask me: In what, then,
does the essence of this unscientific and
unphilosophical knowledge consist? If it
be neither scientific nor philosophical, of
what sort is it? How is it to be defined?
To these questions I can only reply that
as religious knowledge is that which
precedes, and upon which is founded,
every other knowledge, it cannot be
defined, there being no means of definition in existence. In theological language
this knowledge is called revelation. And
this word, if we do not give it any mystic
meaning, is quite accurate; because this
knowledge is not acquired by study, nor
by the efforts of individuals, but through

the reception by them of the manifestation of the Infinite Mind, which, little by little, discloses itself to men.   Why is it that ten thousand years ago men were unable to understand that the meaning of their life was not exhausted by the welfare of the individual, and that later came a time when the higher family-social-State-national conception of life was disclosed to mankind? Why is it that, within the limits of historical memory, the Christian conception of life has been disclosed to men? And why has it been disclosed to such a man or men, and precisely at such a time, at such and no other place, in such and no other form?

To try to answer these questions by searching for their reasons in the historical circumstances of the time, life, and character and special qualities of those men who first accepted and expressed this conception of life, is as though one were to try to prove why the rising sun first casts his rays on certain objects.   The sun of truth, rising higher and higher upon the world, enlightens it ever further, and is reflected by those forms on which first fall the illumination of its rays, and which are most capable of reflecting them.   The qualities which give to some the power of receiving the rising truth are no special activities of the mind, but, on the contrary, are rather passive qualities of the heart, seldom corresponding to a great and inquisitive intellect.   Rejection of the vanities of the world, a sense of one's material frailty, and of truthfulness, are what we observe in every founder of a religion, none of whom have been distinguished by philosophical or scientific acquirement.

In my opinion, the chief error, which, more than all else, impedes the true progress of Christian humanity, is precisely the fact that the scientific men of our time, who are now in the seat of Moses, being guided by the pagan conception of life revived at the Renaissance, and having accepted as the essence of Christianity its crudest distortions, and having decided that it is a condition already outworn by mankind (while they consider, on the contrary, that the ancient social-State conception of paganism, which is indeed outworn, is the loftiest conception and one that should steadfastly be held by humanity), these men not only do not understand true Christianity, which comprises that most perfect conception of life towards which all humanity is advancing, but they do not even try to understand it.

The chief source of this misunderstanding arises from the fact that men of science, having diverged from Christianity, and seen that their science cannot conform to it, have agreed that Christianity and not science must be at fault: that is, they have assumed, not the fact that science is 1800 years behind Christianity, which embraced the greater part of contemporary society, but that it is Christianity which is 1800 years in arrear. From this distortion of facts arises the curious circum-

stance that no people have more entangled
ideas as to the essence of true knowledge,
religion, morality, and existence than men
of science, and the yet more curious fact
that the science of our time, despite all its
successes in examining the phenomena of
the material world, appears to be, as to
human existence, either unnecessary or
productive of merely pernicious results.
And hence I hold that it is neither
philosophy nor science which can determine the relation of man to the universe,
but only religion.

And so I answer your first question, as
to what I understand by the word
"religion," thus—Religion is a certain
relation of man to the eternal, infinite
universe, its origin and source. Out of
this reply to your first question follows
naturally that to the second. If religion
is a definite relation of man to the universe
which determines the meaning of his life,
morality is the index and explanation of
man's activity which naturally flows from
one or other perceived relation. And as
we recognise only two of these perceptions,
if we include the pagan-social as the
enlargement of the personal relation, or
three, if we consider it apart, so there
exist but three moral teachings: the
primitive, savage, individualistic; the
pagan - family - State or social; and the
Christian or godly, teaching man's subservience to the universe or to God.

From the first conception of man's
relationship proceeds the morality common

to all pagan religions whose essential tendency is the welfare of the individual,
and which, therefore, defines every condition capable of producing that welfare
and the means by which it may be pro-
cured.

From this perception of man's relationship have proceeded the pagan moralities;
the Epicurean in its lowest manifestation;
the Mohammedan, promising the welfare of
the individual in this and the next world;
the Church-Christian, with salvation for
its object — that is, the welfare of the
individual chiefly in the world to come;
and the worldly utilitarian, having for its
object the welfare of the individual in this
world alone.

From this same conception, which proclaims the welfare of the individual, and
hence his immunity from pain, as the
object of his existence, proceeds the
Buddhist morality in its crudest aspect and
the worldly teaching of the pessimists.

From the second pagan conception,
which proclaims the welfare of a certain
association of individuals as the object of
existence, proceed those moral teachings
which demand from mankind subservience
to that particular association, the welfare
of which is accepted as the aim of life.
According to this morality, such amount
of personal welfare is alone permitted as
may be procurable for the entire association which forms the religious base of
existence.

From this relation of man to the

universe proceed such moral teachings of
the Greek and Roman world as are known
to us, in which the individual is always
sacrificed to society; the moral teaching of
China; the Jewish morality of personal
subjection to the welfare of the chosen
people; and the Church-State-moral teaching of our own time which demands the
sacrifice of the individual to the welfare of
the State.

From this same conception proceeds also
the morality of the majority of women,
sacrificing their individuality to the
welfare of the family, and especially of
their children. All ancient history, and
in part that of the Middle Ages, and of
the modern era, is full of the exploits
of this family-social and State morality.
And, at the present time, most men only
imagine they profess Christianity and hold
the Christian morality, but in reality they
follow this family - State morality of
paganism. And this morality they elevate
into an ideal in the education of the
young.

From the third conception of man's
relation to the universe—namely, the
acknowledgment by man of his existence
as an instrument of the Supreme Will for
the accomplishment of its designs—proceeds the morality corresponding to this
conception, which explains the dependence
of man on the Supreme Will, and determines the demands of this Will. From
this perception, proceeds the loftiest
morality known to man—the Pythagorean

Stoic, Buddhist, Brahmin, and Taoist—in their best aspects, and the Christian teaching in its real sense, which demands the renunciation of the individual will, and of the welfare, not only of the individual, but of family, society, and State, in the name of the fulfilment of His will who gave us the existence which our consciousness has disclosed.

From one of these perceptions of man's relationship to the infinite universe or its first cause proceeds the true, sincere morality of every man, in spite of what he nominally professes or preaches as morality or the appearance he desires to convey.

So that a man who acknowledges that the essence of his relation to the universe consists in the acquirement of the greatest welfare for himself, however much he may prate of the morality of living for family, society, State, humanity, or the accomplishment of the will of God (though he may be clever enough by feigning to deceive his fellows), the real motive of his activity will always be the welfare of himself, so that, when occasion arises for choice, he will sacrifice, not himself for his family, nation, or the accomplishment of God's will, but everything for himself, because his conception of existence being centred in his own welfare, he cannot act otherwise till the conception of his relation to the universe undergoes a change.

In the same way, however much a man, the conception of whose relation to the universe consists in the service of his

family (as is the case with most women),
tribe, country, or nation (as those of
oppressed nationalities, or political workers
in times of contention), may say that he is
a Christian, his morality will always remain a family, national, or State morality,
not a Christian; and when the necessity
arises for choosing between the welfare of
family or of society and that of himself, or
between social welfare and the accomplishment of God's will, he will inevitably
choose to serve the welfare of that association of his fellows for which he, according
to his conception of life, exists; because
only in such service does he discover the
meaning of his existence.　And, similarly,
however much you may assure a man, who
considers that his relation to the universe
consists in the accomplishment of the Will
of Him that sent him, that he must, in the
interest of person, family, State, nation, or
humanity, do that which contradicts this
Superior Will, of which he is conscious
through the reason and love with which
he is equipped, he will always sacrifice
persons, family, country, or humanity
rather than be unfaithful to the Will of
Him that sent him, because only by the
accomplishment of this Will does he
realise his conception of life.

Morality cannot be independent of religion, because, not only is it the outcome
of religion—that is, of that conception
by man of his relation to the universe
—but because it is already implied by
religion.　All religion is a reply to the

question, What is the meaning of my life?
And the religious answer always includes
a certain moral demand, which may sometimes follow the explanation of this conception, sometimes precede it. The question may be answered thus—The meaning
of life is in the welfare of the individual,
therefore profit by every advantage accessible to thee ; or, The meaning of life
is in the welfare of an association, serve
therefore that association with all thy
power ; or, The meaning of life is in the
fulfilment of the Will of Him that sent
thee, therefore try, with all thy power, to
learn that Will and to do it. And the
same question may be answered thus—
The meaning of thy life is in thy personal
pleasure, and that is the true destiny of
man ; or, The meaning of life is in the
service of that association of which thou
considerest thyself a member, for that is
thy destiny ; or, The meaning of life is in
the service of God, since for that thou
hast been made.

Morality is included in the explanation
of life which religion offers us, and therefore cannot possibly be divorced from it.
This truth is especially evident in those
attempts of non-Christian philosophers to
deduce the inculcation of the loftiest
morality from their philosophy. These
teachers see that Christian morality is
indispensable ; that existence without it
is impossible ; more, they see that such
a morality does exist, and they desire in
some manner to attach it to their non-

Christian philosophy, and even so to represent things that it may appear as if
Christian morality were the natural outcome of their heathen or social philosophy.
And they make the attempt, but their very
efforts exhibit more clearly than anything
else, not only the independence of Christian
morality, but its complete contradiction of
the philosophy of individual welfare, of
escape from personal suffering, of the welfare of society.

Christian ethics, that of which we become conscious by a religious conception
of life, demand not only the sacrifice of
personality to an aggregate of persons, but
of one's own person and any aggregate of
persons to the service of God.   Whereas,
heathen philosophy, investigating the
means by which the welfare of the individual or of an association of individuals
may be achieved, inevitably contradicts
the Christian ideal.   Pagan philosophy
has but one method for concealing this
discrepancy; it heaps up abstract con-
ditional notions, one upon the other, and
refuses to emerge from the misty region
of metaphysics.   Chiefly after this manner
was the behaviour of the philosophers
since the Renaissance, and to this circum-
stance—namely, the impossibility of re-
conciling the demands of Christian morality
already recognised as existing, with philosophy upon a heathen basis — one must
attribute that awful abstraction, unclear-
ness, incomprehensibility, estrangement
from life, of the new philosophy.

With the exception of Spinoza, whose philosophy proceeded from a religious and truly Christian basis, although he is not commonly reckoned a Christian, and of Kant, a gifted genius who resolutely conducted his ethics independent of his metaphysics; with these two exceptions, every other philosopher, even the brilliant Schopenhauer, manifestly devised artificial connections between their ethics and their metaphysics. One feels that Christian ethics have an original and firmly established standpoint independent of philosophy, and needing not at all the fictitious props placed beneath it, and that philosophy invents such statements not only to avoid an appearance of contradiction, but apparently to involve a natural connection and outcome.

But all these statements only seem to justify Christian ethics while they are considered in the abstract. The moment they are fitted to questions of practical existence, then not only does their disagreement become visible in all its force, but the contradiction between the philosophical basis and that which we regard as morality is made manifest. The unhappy Nietzche, who has lately become so celebrated, is especially noticeable as an example of this contradiction. He is irrefutable when he says that all rules of morality, from the standpoint of the existent non-Christian philosophy, are nothing but falsehood and hypocrisy, and that it is much more advantageous, pleasant, and reasonable for

a man to create a society of *Uebermensch,*
and to become one of its members, than
to be one of a crowd which must serve as
a scaffold for that society.

No combinations of philosophy which
proceed from the pagan religious conception of life can prove that it will be of
greater advantage to, and more reasonable
for, a man to live, not for his own desired,
attainable, and conceivable welfare, or for
the welfare of his family and society, but
for the welfare of another, which, as far
as he is concerned, may be undesirable,
inconceivable, and unattainable by his
own insufficient means.   That philosophy
which is founded on man's welfare as the
conception of life can never prove to
a reasoning being, with the ever-present
consciousness of death, that it is fitting
for him to renounce his own desirable,
conceivable, and certain welfare, not for
the certain welfare of others—for he can
never know the results of his sacrifice—
but merely because it is right that he
should do so : that it is the categorical
imperative.

It is impossible to prove this from the
pagan-philosophical standpoint.   In order
to prove that men are all equal, that it is
best for a man to sacrifice his own life in
the service of others, rather than to make
his fellows serve him, trampling upon
their lives, it is necessary for a man to re-
define his relation to the universe, and to
understand that such is the position of
a man that he is left no other course,

because the meaning of his life is only to be found in the accomplishment of the Will of Him that sent him, and that the Will of Him that sent him is—that he should give his life to the service of mankind. And such a modification in man's perception of his relation to the universe is wrought only by religion.

So, too, is it with the attempts to deduce Christian morality from, and to harmonise it with, the fundamental propositions of pagan science. No sophisms nor mental shifting will destroy the simple and clear proposition, that the hypothesis of evolution, laid as the basis of all the science of our time, is founded upon a general, unchangeable, and eternal law —that of the struggle for existence, and of the survival of the "fittest"—and that, therefore, every man, for the attainment of his own welfare, or of that of his society, must be this fittest, or make his society the fittest, in order that neither he nor his society should perish, but another less fit. However much some naturalists, alarmed by the logical inferences of this law, and by its adaptation to human existence, may strive to extinguish it with words and talk it down, its irrefutability becomes only the more manifest by their efforts, and its control over the life of the entire organic world, and hence over that of man, regarded as an animal.

While I am writing this,[1] the Russian translation of an article by Professor

[1] 1894.

Huxley has been published, compiled from a speech of his upon the evolution of ethics before a certain English society. In this article the learned Professor—as did some years ago, too, our eminent Professor Beketoff as unsuccessfully as his predecessors—tries to prove that the struggle for existence does not violate morality, and that, alongside the acceptance of the law of this struggle as the fundamental law of existence, morality may not only exist, but may improve. Mr. Huxley's article is full of a variety of jokes, verses, and general views upon the religion and philosophy of the ancients, and therefore is so shock-headed and entangled that only with great pains can one arrive at the fundamental idea. This, however, is as follows :—The law of evolution is contrary to the law of morality ; this was known to the ancient world of Greece and India. And the philosophy and religion of either nation led them to the teaching of self-abnegation. This teaching, according to the author's opinion, is not correct ; but the right one is the following : A law exists, termed by the author "cosmic," according to which all creatures struggle amongst themselves, and only the fittest survives. Man is subordinate to this law, and, thanks to it, has became what he now is. But this law is contrary to morality. How, then, are we to reconcile morality with this law ? Thus : Social progress exists which tends to suspend the cosmic process, and to replace it by another—an

3

ethical one, the object of which is no
longer the survival of the "fittest," but of
the "best" in the ethical sense.

Whence came this ethical process Mr.
Huxley does not explain, but in Note 19
he says that the basis of this process
consists in the fact that men, as well as
animals, prefer, on the one hand, to live in
companies, and therefore smother within
themselves those propensities which are
pernicious to societies, and, on the other
hand, the members of societies crush by
force such actions as are prejudicial to the
welfare of the society. Mr. Huxley thinks
that this process, which compels men to
control their passions for the preservation
of that association to which they belong,
and the fear of punishment should they
break the rules of that association, compose that very ethical process the existence
of which it behoves him to prove. It
evidently appears to the mind of Mr.
Huxley, that in English society of our
time, with its Irish destitution, its insane
luxury of the rich, its trade in opium
and spirits, its executions, its sanguinary
wars, its extermination of entire nations
for the sake of commerce and policy, its
secret vice and hypocrisy—it evidently
appears to him that a man who does not
overstep police regulations is a moral man,
and that such a man is guided by an
ethical process. Mr. Huxley seems to
forget that qualities which may be needful
to prevent the destruction of that society
in which its member lives, may be of

service to the society itself ; and that the personal qualities of the members of a band of brigands are also useful to the band ; as, also, in our society, we find a use for hangmen, jailers, judges, soldiers, false pastors, etc., but that these qualities have nothing in common with morality.

Morality is an affair of constant development and growth, and hence the preservation of the instituted orders of a certain society, by means of the rope and scaffold, to which as instruments of morality Mr. Huxley alludes, will be not only not the confirmation, but the infraction of morality. And, on the contrary, every infringement of existing canons, such as was the violation by Christ and His disciples of the ordinances of a Roman province, such as would be the defiance of existing regulations by a man who refuses to take part in judgments at law, military service, and payment of taxes, used for military preparations, will be not only not contrary to morality, but the indispensable condition of its manifestation. Every cannibal, who ceases to partake of his species, acts in the same manner and transgresses the ordinances of his society. Hence though actions which infringe the regulations of society may be immoral, without doubt, also, every truly moral action which advances the cause of morality is always achieved by transgressing some ordinance of society. And, therefore, if there has ever appeared in a society a law which demands the sacrifice of personal advantage to preserve the unity

of the whole social fabric, that law is not
an ethical statute, but, for the most part,
on the contrary (being opposed to all
ethics), is that same law of struggle for
existence in a latent and concealed form.
It is the same struggle, but transferred
from units to their agglomerations.   It is
not the cessation of strife, but the swinging
backward of the arm to hit the stronger.
If the law of the struggle for existence
and survival of the fittest is the eternal
law of all life (and one must perforce
regard it as such with reference to man
considered as an animal), then such misty
arguments as to social progress—supposed
to proceed from it, and arisen none knows
whence, a *deus ex machinâ* ethical process
to assist us in our need—cannot break
that law down.   If social progress, as Mr.
Huxley assures us, collects men into
groups, then the same struggle and the
same survival will exist between families,
races, and States, and this struggle will be,
not only not more moral, but more cruel
and immoral than that between individuals,
as, indeed, we find it in reality.

Even if we admit the impossible—that
all humanity, solely by social progress,
will in a thousand years achieve a single
unity and will be of one State and nation,
even then, not to mention that the struggle
suppressed between States and nations
will be altered to one between humanity
and the animal world, and that that
struggle will always remain a struggle—
that is, an activity absolutely excluding

the possibility of Christian morality as
professed by us—not to speak of this, the
struggle between the individuals which
compose this unity, and between the
associations of families, races, nationalities
will not in the least be diminished, but will
continue the same, only in another form,
as we may observe in all associations of
men in families, races, and States. Those
of one family quarrel and fight—and often
more and most cruelly—between themselves, as well as with strangers. So also
in a State, the same struggle continues
between those within it, as between them
and those without, only in other forms.
In one case men kill each other with
arrows and knives, in another by starva-
tion. And if the feeblest are sometimes
preserved in the family or State, it is in
no wise thanks to the State association,
but because self-abnegation and tenderness
exist among people joined in families and
States. If, of two children without
parents, only the fittest survives, the fact
that both might live with the help of
a good mother, will not be a consequence of family unification, but because a
certain mother is gifted with tenderness
and self-denial. And neither of these
gifts can proceed from social progress. To
assert that social progress produces morality
is equivalent to saying that the erection of
stoves produces heat. Heat proceeds from
the sun; and stoves produce heat only
when fuel — the work of the sun —
is kindled in them; so morality pro-

ceeds from religion, and social forms of
life produce morality only when into these
forms are put the results of religious
influence on humanity—this is, morality.
Stoves may be kindled, and so may impart
heat, or may be left unlit and so remain
cold. So, too, social forms may include
morality, and in that case morally influence
society, or may not include morality and
thus remain without influence. Christian
morality cannot be founded on the heathen
or social conception of life, nor can it be
deduced either from non-Christian philosophy or science—can not only not be
deduced, but cannot be reconciled with
them. So always was it understood by all
serious, consistent, ancient philosophy and
science, which said, "Do our propositions
disagree with morality? Well, then, so
much the worse for morality," and continued their investigations.

Ethical treatises not founded on religion,
and even lay catechisms, are written and
taught, and men may believe that humanity
is guided by them; but it only seems to
be so, because people in reality are guided,
not by these treatises and catechisms, but
by the religion which they have always
had and have; whereas the treatises and
catechisms only try to counterfeit the
natural outflux of religion. Ordinances of
lay morality not founded upon religious
teaching are similar to the actions of a
man who, being ignorant of music, should
take the conductor's seat before the
orchestra, and begin to wave his arms

before the musicians, who are performing. The music might continue a little while by its own momentum, and from the previous knowledge of the players, but it is evident that the mere waving of a stick by a man who is ignorant of music would be not only useless, but would inevitably confuse the musicians and disorganise the orchestra in the end. The same disorder is beginning to take place in the minds of the men of our time, in consequence of the attempts of leading men to teach people morality, not founded on that loftiest religion which is in process of adoption, and is in part adopted by Christian humanity. It would be, indeed, desirable to have a moral teaching unmixed with superstition, but the fact is that moral teaching is only the result of a certain defined relation of man to the universe, or to God. If the determination of such a relation is expressed in forms which seem to us superstitious, then, in order to prevent this, we should try to express this relation more clearly, reasonably, and accurately, and even to destroy the former perception of man's relationship which has become insufficient, and to put in its place one loftier, clearer, and more reasonable; but by no means to invent a so-called lay, irreligious morality founded on sophisms, or upon nothing at all.

The attempts to found a morality independent of religion are like the actions of children when, wishing to move a plant which pleases them, they tear off the root which does not please and seems unnecessary to them, and plant it in the earth without the root. Without a religious foundation there can be no true, unsimulated morality, as without a root there can be no true plant. And so in reply to your two questions, I say religion is man's conception of his relation to the infinite universe, and to its source. And morality is the ever-present guide of life proceeding only from this relation.

PRINTED BY
MORRISON AND GIBB LIMITED, EDINBURGH

Some Social Remedies

Socialism, Anarchy
Land Nationalisation
Communism, etc.

By Leo Tolstoy

The Free Age Press
1900

The Free Age Press stands for an attempt to assist in spreading those deep convictions in which the noblest spirits of every age and race have united—that man's true aim and happiness is "unity in reason and love"; the realisation of the brotherhood of all men,—and that we *must* all strive to purge away, each from himself, those false ideas, false feelings, and false desires, personal, social, religious, political, racial, economic, which alienate us one from another and produce nine-tenths of the sum of human suffering.

Of these truly Christian and universally religious aspirations the writings of Leo Tolstoy are perhaps to-day the most definite expression, and it is for the production of 1d., 3d., and 6d. editions of all his known religious, social, and ethical works, together with the unpublished matter and future writings to which we have and shall have special access (being in close relationship with Tolstoy), that *The Free Age Press* will at first devote itself; trusting that all who sympathise will assist by every means in their power, especially in helping to spread the books the world over, losing no opportunity of introducing them whenever and wherever feasible, and of so making it possible for the work to be continued, and extended into wider and wider fields. As it is Tolstoy's desire that his books shall not be copyrighted, our editions will, whenever possible, be free to the world.

Suggestions, criticisms, inquiries, offers of help and co-operation will be gratefully welcomed; and it is specially requested that the names of any books that have helped towards a better understanding of life may be furnished, so that a much-needed list may be compiled and published.

Letters, Private Orders, and Money Orders (it is hoped that friends will *purchase* as many copies as possible; even one will help) should be addressed to THE EDITORS, "FREE AGE PRESS," MALDON, ESSEX. *Booksellers* must order from Messrs. SIMPKIN, MARSHALL, HAMILTON, KENT & Co. LTD., London, E.C.; THE CLARION CO. LTD., 72 Fleet Street, E.C.; Messrs. JOHN MENZIES & Co., Glasgow; and Mr. JOHN HEYWOOD, Manchester.

SOME SOCIAL REMEDIES

Uniform with "Some Social Remedies."

Long 8vo, sewed, 3d. each ; post free, 3½d.

Patriotism and Government. Leo
Tolstoy.

Thoughts on God. Leo Tolstoy.

On the Personal Christian Life.
Leo Tolstoy.

Letters on War. Leo Tolstoy.

Religion and Morality. Leo Tolstoy.

———

In Preparation.

The Relation of the Sexes. Leo
Tolstoy.

Education of Children. Leo Tolstoy.

Conceptions of Life. Leo Tolstoy.

Christian Anarchy. Leo Tolstoy.

SOME SOCIAL

REMEDIES . .

SOCIALISM, ANARCHY, .
HENRY GEORGISM AND .
THE LAND QUESTION, .
COMMUNISM, Etc. . .

COLLECTED FROM
THE RECENT AND
UNPUBLISHED .
WRITINGS OF . .
LEO . . . .
TOLSTOY .

THE FREE AGE PRESS
CHRISTCHURCH, HANTS . .
(New Address)

1900

SOME SOCIAL REMEDIES

SOCIALISM, STATE AND CHRISTIAN —
ANARCHY — HENRY GEORGISM AND
THE LAND QUESTION — COMMUNISM,
ETC.

ON SOCIALISM, STATE AND CHRISTIAN
(From the Private MS. Diary)

"LOOKING Backward" is excellent. One
thing is bad, namely, the Socialist, Marx-
ian idea that if one does wrong for a
very long time, good will ensue of its own
accord. "Capital is accumulated in the
hands of a few ; it will end by being held
by one. All trades-unions will be also
united into one. There are capital and
labour,—divided. Authority or revolution will unite them, and all will be
well." The chief point is that nothing
in our civilisation will diminish, nothing
recede ; there will be the same mansions,
the same gastronomic dinners, sweets,
wines, carriages, horses,—only everything
will be accessible to all.

It is incomprehensible that they do not
see this to be impossible. Take for instance the luxuries of the house of

5

Yasnaia Poliana, and divide them among the peasants. It can't be done. They would be of no use to them. Luxury must be given up. Nothing will do so long as violence, capital, and invention are directed towards that which is unnecessary. And in order to get at what is necessary for the masses, everything must be tested.

But the chief thing is that we must be ready to renounce all the improvements of our civilisation, rather than allow those cruel inequalities which constitute our scourge. If I really love my brother, then I shall not hesitate to deprive myself of a drawing-room, in order to shelter him when he is homeless. As it is, we say that we wish to shelter our brother, but only on condition that our drawing-rooms remain free for receptions. We must decide whom we will serve—God or mammon. To serve both is impossible. If we are to serve God, we must be prepared to give up luxury and civilisation; being ready to introduce them again to-morrow, but only for the common and equal use of all.

.   .   .   .   .

The most profitable social arrangement (economic and otherwise) is one in which each thinks of the good of all, and devotes himself unreservedly to the service of that welfare. If all were so disposed, each would derive the greatest possible amount of good.

The most unprofitable grouping of

people (economically and otherwise) is
that in which each works for himself
only, depends and provides for himself
only. If this were universally the case,
if there were not at least family groups
in which people work for one another, I
do not think men could live.

However, people have not this yearning
for the welfare of others; on the contrary,
each is striving for his own welfare, to
the detriment of others. But this state
of things is so unprofitable that men
speedily grow weak in the struggle. And
now, by the very nature of things, it
occurs that one man overpowers others
and makes them serve him. And the
result is a more profitable labour of men
instead of the unprofitable individual one.

But in such associations of men there
appear inequality and oppression. And
therefore people are making attempts at
equalisation (such as the attempts at co-
operations, communes) and at the liberation of men (such as political rights).
Equalisation always leads to disadvantage
of the work done. In order to equalise
the remuneration, the best workman is
brought down to the level of the worst;
things in use are divided in such a manner
that no one may have more, or better,
than another, as in the partition of land;
and this is why the divisions of land are
being made smaller and smaller, a practice
disadvantageous to all. Liberation from
oppression by political rights is leading to
even greater excitement and ill-will. Thus

attempts at equalisation and deliverance from oppression are made, though without success; while the unification, the subjugation of ever greater and greater numbers of men by one is always increasing. The greater the centralisation of labour the more profitable it is, but also the more striking and revolting is the inequality.

What, then, is to be done? Individual labour is unprofitable; centralised labour is more profitable, but the inequality and oppression are terrible.

Socialists wish to remove inequality and oppression by assigning all capital to the nation, to humanity, so that the centralised unit will become humanity itself. But, in the first place, not only humanity, but even nations do not as yet admit the necessity for this, and until they do, this system cannot be adopted by all humanity; secondly, among men striving each for his own welfare, it would be impossible to find men sufficiently disinterested to manage the capital of humanity without taking advantage of their power—men who would not again introduce into the world inequality and oppression.

And so humanity stands unavoidably face to face with this dilemma: either the forward movement attained by the centralisation of labour must be renounced, —there must even be retrogression rather than an infringement of equality or allowance of oppression,—or else it should be boldly admitted that inequality and oppression must exist, that "when wood

is chopped, splinters will fly," that there
must be victims, and that struggle is the
law of humanity. And this view is, in
fact, adopted and supported by certain
people. But, side by side with it, there
resounds ever louder and louder the
protests of the dispossessed, the moans
of the oppressed and the voices of the
indignant raised in the name of the ideal
of Christ, of truth and good; which ideal is
acknowledged by our society only officially.

But any child can see that the greatest
advantage would result to all if everyone
were to interest himself in the common
cause, and therefore to be provided for as
a member of the whole. As, however,
this is not the practice, as it is impossible
to enter into the soul of everyone and
control it, and as to persuade everybody
is also impossible, or would take infinitely
long, there remains but one other course:
to assist the centralisation of labour,
resulting from the subjugation of the
many by the few, and at the same time
to conceal from the dispossessed their
inequality with the fortunate, to ward off
their attacks, and to help and afford
charity to the oppressed. And this is
being done; but the concentration of
capital increases more and more, and the
inequality and oppression grow ever more
cruel. And side by side with this,
enlightenment becomes more general and
the inequality and the cruelty of oppression more evident both to oppressed and
oppressors.

Further movement in this direction is becoming impossible; so those who think little, who do not look to the logical conclusion, propose imaginary remedies, consisting in the education of men in the consciousness of the necessity of co-operation for the sake of greater advantage. This is absurd. If the aim be great advantage, then everyone will get this advantage for himself in the capitalistic organisations. And therefore nothing except talk results from these attempts.

The organisation most profitable for all will be attained not while everyone's aim is profit, material welfare, but only when the aim of all is that welfare which is independent of earthly well-being—when everyone will say from his heart, "Blessed are the poor; blessed are those that weep, those who are persecuted." Only when everyone seeks, not material but spiritual welfare, which always coincides with sacrifice, is verified by sacrifice—only then will result the greatest welfare for all.

Take this simple illustration: People live together; if they tidy up regularly, clean up after themselves, everyone has to do very little in order to preserve the general cleanliness. But everyone is accustomed to have things tidied and cleaned up after him; what, then, has he to do who wishes to keep the place clean? He must work for all, must be immersed in dirt. And if he will not do this, will

work only for himself, he will not attain
his aim. Of course it would be easier to,
order all the others; but there is no one
who can so order. There remains but one
course—oneself to work for others.

And, indeed, in a world where all are living for themselves, to begin to live for others
a little is impossible; one must give oneself up entirely. And it is just this that
the conscience, enlightened by Christ,
demands.

`   Why is it that the kingdom of God upon
earth can be realised neither by means of
the existing governmental violence nor by
a revolution and State Socialism, nor yet
by those means preached by Christian
Socialists: propaganda and the gradually
increasing consciousness of men that it will
be advantageous?

So long as Man's aim is the welfare of
the personal life, no one can check himself
in this strife for his-welfare at the point
where he gets his just share,—and at such
demands from men which admit of the
well-being of all. No one can do this,
firstly, because it is impossible to find the
point of perfect justice in these requests,—
men will always exaggerate their demands;
and secondly, because, even were it possible to find the measure of the just demands,
man cannot put forward the demand for
that which is only just, for he will never
get it, but infinitely less. The demands of
those around him being regulated, not by
justice, but by personal profit, it is evident

that as a matter of fact the possession of material welfare will be attained by every separate individual rather through competition and struggle (as indeed is at present the case) than by just demands.

In order to attain justice, while people are striving after personal welfare, it would be necessary to have people able to define the measure of worldly goods which should in justice fall to the share of each; and also people with power to prevent men profiting by more than their just share. There are, and always have been, men who have undertaken both these duties; they are our rulers.   But up to the present time neither in monarchies nor in republics have there been found men who, in defining the measure of goods and distributing them amongst men, have not transgressed this measure for themselves and their assistants, and thus *spoilt the work they were called to, and undertook to do.*   So that this means is already recognised by all to be unsatisfactory.   And now some people say that it is necessary to abolish these governments and to establish governments of another kind, chiefly for the purpose of superintending economic affairs,—which governments, acknowledging that all capital and land are common property, will administer the labour of men and distribute earthly welfare, according to their labour,—or, as some say, according to their needs.

All attempts at this kind of organisation, hitherto made, have been unsuccessful.

But even without such experiments, one can confidently assert that, with men striving after personal welfare, such an organisation cannot be realised, because those men —very many of them—who will superintend economic affairs, will be men with strivings after personal welfare, and will have to deal with similar men, and therefore in organising and maintaining the new economic order, they will inevitably prosecute their own personal advantage as much as the former administrators, and will thus destroy the meaning of the very work they are called to do.

Some will say, "Choose men who are wise and pure." But none but the wise and pure can choose the wise and pure. And if all men were wise and pure, there would be no need of any organisation, consequently the impossibility of that which the revolutionary Socialists profess is felt by all, even by themselves; and that is why it is out of date and has no success.

And here we come to the third teaching —that of Christian Socialism, which has resource to propaganda aiming at influencing the consciousness of men. But the success of this teaching is evidently possible only when all men will have the same clear consciousness of the advantages of community of labour, and when this consciousness will have simultaneously developed in all. But as it is evident that neither the one nor the other can take place, the economic organisation founded, not on competition and struggle, but on community of interest cannot be realised.

Therefore there cannot be a better organisation than the present one, so long as the aim of man is personal welfare.

The error of those who preach Christian Socialism consists in this, that they draw from the Gospels only that practical conclusion of general welfare which is not the aim pointed out by the Gospels, but only the verification of the correctness of the means. The Gospels teach the way of life, and by advancing on this way it happens that material welfare is reached. It is indeed attained, but it is not the aim. If the aim of the gospel teaching were limited to the attainment of material welfare, then this material welfare would not be attained.

The aim is higher and more distant. The aim of this teaching is not dependent on material welfare; it is the salvation of the soul, *i.e.* of that divine element which has been enclosed in man. This salvation is attained by renouncing personal life and therefore, also, material well-being, and by striving after the welfare of one's neighbours—by love. And it is only by this endeavour that men will, incidentally, attain the greatest welfare of all—the kingdom of God upon earth.

By striving after personal welfare, neither personal nor general welfare is attained. By striving after self-forgetfulness, both personal and general welfare are attained.

Theoretically, three organisations of

human society are possible. The first is
this : people—the best people, God's—will
give such a law to men as will ensure the
greatest happiness to mankind, and the
authorities will enforce the fulfilment of
this law. This has been tried ; but has
resulted in the authorities, those who administered the law, abusing their power
and infringing the law, not they only but
also their co-operators, who are many.
Then appeared a second scheme, " *Laisser
faire, laisser passer*," the idea being that
there is no need of authorities, but that by
all men striving each for his own welfare,
justice will be realised. But this does
not succeed for two reasons. Firstly,
because authority is not abolished, and
people think it cannot be abolished because
oppression would still continue, for the
government would refuse to use its authority
to arrest the robber, whereas the robber
would not desist. While there are authorities the condition of men fighting for
welfare is unequal, not only because some
are stronger than others, but also because
men make use of authority to help them in
the struggle. Secondly, because in the
incessant struggle of all, each for his own
welfare, the slightest advantage of one
gives him a multiplied advantage, and inequality must inevitably result. There
still remains a third theory, that men will
come to understand that it is profitable to
live for the welfare of others, and that all
will strive after this. And it is just this
that the Christian faith furnishes. In the

first place, to the realisation of this theory there can be no external obstacles; whether or not there exist government, capital, etc., and the whole present order of things, the object would be attained in the event of such a development of men's conception of life. Secondly, one need expect no special term for the commencement of the realisation, for every single individual who has attained this life conception, and gives himself up to the welfare of others, is already conducing to that welfare. And thirdly, this has been going on ever since we have known anything about the life of men.

.   .   .   .   .

Socialists say, "It is not necessary for us who enjoy the blessings of culture and civilisation to be deprived of these blessings, and to descend to the level of the rough crowd, but the men who are now deprived of material good must be raised to our level, and made participators in the blessings of culture and civilisation. The means for accomplishing this is science. Science teaches us to conquer nature; it is able infinitely to increase the productiveness of nature; it may by electricity avail itself of the power of the Niagara Falls, of rivers, of winds. The sun will work. And there will be plenty of everything for everybody. At present only a small fraction of mankind, the one in power, profits by the blessings of civilisation; whereas the rest is deprived of them. Increase the welfare, and then it will suffice for all." But the fact is that those in power have long been consuming not what they need, but what they do not need; all they can get. Therefore, however much advantages may increase, those who are at the top will appropriate them for themselves.

One cannot consume more than a certain quantity of necessaries, but to luxury there is no limit. Thousands of bushels of bread may be used for horses and dogs; millions of acres of land turned into parks, and so on, as is now the case. So that no increase of productiveness and wealth will augment one tittle the welfare of the lower classes, so long as the upper classes have the power and the desire to spend the surplus wealth on luxury. On the contrary, the increase of productiveness, the greater mastery of the forces of nature, only gives greater power to the upper classes, to those in authority,—power to keep this authority over the lower working classes.

And every attempt on the part of the lower classes to make the rich divide with them,—revolutions, strikes,—cause strife, and the strife—a useless waste of wealth. "Better let no one have it, if I cannot,' say the contending parties.

The conquest of nature and the increased production of material wealth in order that it may overflow the world, so that every one may have his share, is as unwise a proceeding as would be to increase the quantity of wood thrown into a stove, in order

2

to increase the warmth of a house in which
the stoves have no dampers. However
much you may augment the fire, the cold
air becoming heated will rise, and fresh
cold air will at once take its place ; and
therefore no equal distribution of warmth
in the house will be attained. This will
continue as long as there is access for the
cold air and an outlet for the hot.

Of the three remedies which have so
far been invented, it is difficult to say
which is the most foolish,—so foolish are
they all.

The first remedy, that of the revolu-
tionist, consists in the abolition of the
upper classes, by whom all the wealth is
consumed. This is the same as if a man
were to break the chimney through which
the heat is disappearing, supposing that
when there is no chimney the heat will
not pass away. But the heat will pass
out through the hole left by the chimney,
as it did through the chimney itself, if the
current be the same. In the same way
wealth will all go to the men in authority,
as long as authority exists.

Another remedy, at present being put
into practice by Wilhelm II., is, without
changing the existing order, to take from
the upper classes, who possess the wealth
and power, a small portion of this wealth
and throw it into the bottomless abyss of
poverty ; as if one were to arrange on the
top of the chimney, through which the
heat is passing, fans, and to fan the heat,
trying to drive it down to the cold layers.

An occupation obviously difficult and useless, because, while the heat ascends from
below, however much one may drive it
down (and one cannot drive down much),
it will at once again rise up and all the
exertion will be wasted.

The third, and last, remedy is at present
preached especially in America. It consists in replacing the competitive and individualistic basis of life by a communistic
principle, by a principle of associations,
co-operations. This remedy, as stated in
Dawn and the *Nationalist*, consists in
preaching co-operation by word and deed,
in inculcating and explaining to men that
competition, individualism, and strife are
destroying much strength and consequently
wealth, and that far greater advantage is
derived from the co-operative principle,
i.e. every one working for the common
good, and receiving afterwards his share
of the common wealth,—that this will
prove more advantageous for everybody.
All this is excellent, but the worst of it is
that, to begin with, no one knows what
each man's share will be when all is
divided equally; and above all, whatever
his share may be, it will appear insufficient
for their welfare to men living as they do
at present. "All will be well off, and
you will enjoy the same as the others."—
"But I don't want to live like all the
rest, I want to live better. I have always
lived better than others and am used to
it."—"And as for me I have long lived
worse than all, and now want to live just

as others have lived." This remedy is the worst of all, because it supposes that during the existing upward current, *i.e.* the motive of striving after the best, it is possible to persuade the particles of air not to rise in proportion to the heat.

The one means is to reveal to men their true welfare, and to show them that wealth not only is not a blessing, but even diverts men from welfare, by hiding from them their true welfare.

There is only one means, and that is to stop up the hole of worldly desire. This alone would give equally distributed heat. And this is exactly the opposite of what the Socialists say and do,—trying to augment production, and therefore the general mass of wealth.

.　　.　　.　　.　　.

Gronlund is arguing with Spencer and all those who deny the need of government, or see its destination only in the security of the individual. Gronlund considers that the foundation of morality lies in association. As a model, or rather as an embryo, of a real socialistic government, he brings forward trades-unions, which, by coercing the individual, by inducing him to sacrifice his personal interests, subordinate him to the service of the common cause.

This, I think, is not true. He says that the government organises labour. That would be well; but he forgets that governments are always coercing and exploiting labour under the pretext of defence. How much more would it then exploit labour under the pretext of organising it? It would indeed be well if government were to organise labour, but to do that it must be disinterested, saintly. But where are they, these saints?,

It is true that individualism, as they call it, meaning by this the ideal of individual welfare for each separate man, is a most pernicious principle; but the principle of the welfare of many people together is equally pernicious. Only its perniciousness is not at once evident.

The attainment of that co-operation— social communism,—in place of individualism, will not result from organisation. We shall never guess what will be the organisation of the future; we will discover it only by everyone following the unperverted impulse of heart, conscience, reason, faith; the law of life, call it what you will.

Bees and ants live socially, not because they know what organisation is most advantageous for them and follow it,— they have no idea of expediency, harmony, the wisdom of the hive or ant hill, as they appear to us, but because they give themselves up to what we call the instinct inherent in them, they submit, not philosophising cunningly, but straightforwardly to their law of life. I can imagine that if bees, in addition to their instinct, as we call it, in addition to the consciousness of their law, were able to invent the best organisation of their social life, they would invent such a life that they would perish.

In this tendency of the law of life there is something less and something more than reasoning. And it alone leads to that way of truth, which is the right one for man and for humanity.

_____

On Anarchy

(*From the Private MS. Diary*)

The Anarchists are right in everything; in the negation of the existing order, and in the assertion that, without authority, there could not be worse violence than that of authority under existing conditions. They are mistaken only in thinking that Anarchy can be instituted by a revolution. "To establish Anarchy." "Anarchy will be instituted." But it will be instituted only by there being more and more people who do not require protection from governmental power, and by there being more and more people who will be ashamed of applying this power.

"The capitalistic organisation will pass into the hands of workers, and then there will be no more oppression of these workers, and no unequal distribution of earnings."

"But who will establish the works; who will administer them?"

"It will go on of its own accord; the workmen themselves will arrange everything."

"But the capitalistic organisation was established just because, for every practical affair, there is need for administrators furnished with power. If there be work there will be leadership, administrators with power. And when there is power there will be abuse of it—the very thing against which you are now striving."

.　　　.　　　.　　　.

To the question, how to be without a State, without courts, armies, so on, an answer cannot be given, because the question is badly formulated. The problem is not how to arrange a State after the pattern of to-day, or after a new pattern. Neither I, nor any of us, is appointed to settle that question.

But, though voluntarily, yet inevitably must we answer the question, How shall I act in face of the problem which ever arises before me? Am I to submit my conscience to the acts taking place around me, am I to proclaim myself in agreement with the government, which hangs erring men, sends soldiers to murder, demoralises nations with opium and spirits, and so on, or am I to submit my actions to conscience, *i.e.* not participate in government, the actions of which are contrary to my reason?

What will be the outcome of this, what kind of a government there will be,—of all this I know nothing ; not that I don't wish to know ; but that I cannot. I only know that nothing evil can result from my following the higher guidance of wisdom and love, or wise love, which is implanted in me; just as nothing evil comes of the bee following the instinct implanted in her, and flying out of the hive with the swarm, we should say, to ruin.   But, I repeat, I do not wish to and cannot judge about this.

In this precisely consists the power of Christ's teaching and that not because, Christ is God or a great man, but because His teaching is irrefutable.   The merit of His teaching consists in the fact that it transferred the matter from the domain of eternal doubt and conjecture on to the ground of certainty.   " Thou art a man, a being rational and kind, and thou knowest that these qualities are the highest in thee; and, besides, thou knowest that to-day or to-morrow thou wilt die, disappear.   If there be a God, then thou wilt go to Him, and He will ask of thee an account of thy actions, whether thou hast acted in accordance with His law, or, at least, with the higher qualities implanted in thee.   If there be no God, thou regardest reason and love as the highest qualities, and must submit to them thy other inclinations, and not let them submit to thy animal nature —to the cares about the commodities of life, to the fear of annoyance, and material calamities."

The question is not, I repeat, which community will be the more secure, the better,—the one which is defended by arms, cannons, gallows, or the one that is not so safeguarded.   But there is only one question for a man, and one it is impossible to evade: "Wilt thou, a rational and good being, having for a moment appeared in this world, and at any moment liable to disappear,—wilt thou take part in the murder of erring men or men of a different race, wilt thou participate in the exterminating of whole nations of so-called savages, wilt thou participate in the artificial deterioration of generations of men by means of opium and spirits for the sake of profit, wilt thou participate in all these actions, or even be in agreement with those who permit them, or wilt thou not?"

And there can be but one answer to this question for those to whom it has presented itself. As to what the outcome will be of it I don't know, because it is not given me to know. But what should be done I do unmistakably know.

And if you ask: "What will happen?" Then I reply that good will certainly happen; because, acting in the way indicated by reason and love, I am acting in accordance with the highest law known to me.

.   .   .   .   .

The situation of the majority of men, enlightened by true brotherly enlightenment, at present crushed by the deceit and cunning of usurpers, who are forcing them to ruin their own lives—this situation is terrible, and appears hopeless.

Only two issues present themselves, and both are closed. One is to destroy violence by violence, by terrorism, dynamite bombs,

gress. "I know what conscience dictates to me; as to you men, occupied with the State, organise the State as best you may, so that it correspond to the demands of the conscience of the men of our time."

But men are abandoning this impregnable position, taking up the view of reforming, ameliorating the State functions; and, by so doing, they are losing their points of support, acknowledging the necessity for the State, and thus abandoning their unassailable position.

.   .   .   .   .

THREE METHODS OF REFORM
(*From the Private MS. Diary*)

There are three means of alleviating the condition of the labourers and of setting up brotherhood among men.

1. Not to make people work for you; neither directly nor indirectly to demand work of them; not to need such articles as demand extra labour,—all objects of luxury.

2. To do for oneself and, *if possible*, for others also that work which is tedious and unpleasant.

3. Not in reality a means, but the result and application of the second, to study the laws of nature and invent processes for the alleviation of labour—machinery, steam, electricity. One will invent what is really needed, and nothing superfluous, *only* when one invents in order to lighten

one's own labour, or at least labour which one has oneself experienced.

But at present men are engaged in applying only the third means, and even that incorrectly, for they keep aloof from the second, and not only are they unwilling to employ the first and second means, but they do not wish even to hear of them.

. . . . .

There can be only one permanent revolution—a moral one ; the regeneration of the inner man.

How is this revolution to take place? Nobody knows how it will take place in humanity, but every man feels it clearly in himself. And yet in our world everybody thinks of changing humanity, and nobody thinks of changing himself.

. . . . .

People abolished slavery and the right of owning slaves, but they continued changing their linen unnecessarily, and living in ten rooms and having five courses at dinner, and carriages, etc. And yet all these things could not be if there were no slaves. This is perfectly clear, and yet nobody can see it.

———

Two Letters on Henry George and the Land Question.

(The first written to a German reformer, who had asked for an expression of opinion on Henry George; and the second, to a Russian peasant in Siberia, who had heard something of Henry George and wished to know more.)

I.

In reply to your letter I send you the enclosed with special pleasure. I have been acquainted with Henry George since the appearance of his *Social Problems*. I read them, and was struck by the correctness of his main idea, and by the unique clearness and power of his argument, which is unlike anything in scientific literature, and especially by the Christian spirit, which also stands alone in the literature of science, which pervades the book. After reading it I turned to his previous work, *Progress and Poverty*, and with a heightened appreciation of its author's activity. You ask my opinion of Henry George's work, and of his single tax system. My opinion is the following :—

Humanity advances continually towards the enlightenment of its consciousness, and to the institution of modes of life corresponding to this consciousness. Hence in every period of life and humanity there is, on the one hand, a progressive enlightenment of consciousness, and on the other a realisation in life of what is enlightened. At the close of the 18th century and the

beginning of the 19th, a progressive enlightenment of consciousness occurred in
Christianised humanity with respect to
the working classes, who were previously in
various phases of slavery; and a progressive realisation of new forms of life—the
abolition of slavery and the substitution
of free-hired labour.

At the present day a progressive enlightenment of human consciousness is
taking place with reference to the use of
land, and soon, it seems to me, a progressive realisation of this must follow. And
in this progressive enlightenment with
reference to the use of land, and its
realisation, which constitutes one of the
chief problems of our time, the fore-man,
the leader of the movement, was and is
Henry George. In this lies his immense
and predominant importance. He con-
tributed by his excellent books both to
the enlightenment of the consciousness of
mankind and to the placing of it upon a
practical footing.

But with the abolition of the revolting
right of ownership in land, the same thing
is being repeated which took place, as we
can still remember, when slavery was
abolished. The governments and ruling
classes, knowing that the advantages and
authority of their position amongst men
are bound up in the land question, while
pretending that they are preoccupied with
the welfare of the people, organising
working-men's banks, inspection of labour,
income taxes, and even an eight hours'

day, studiously ignore the land question, and even, with the aid of an obliging and easily corrupted science, assert that the expropriation of land is useless, harmful, impossible.

The same thing is happening now as in the days of the slave trade. Mankind, at the beginning of the 18th and at the end of the 19th century, had long felt that slavery was an awful, soul-nauseating anachronism; but sham-religion and sham-science proved that there was nothing wrong in it; that it was indispensable, or, at least, that its abolition would be premature. To-day something similar is taking place with reference to property in land. In the same way sham-religion and sham-science are proving that there is nothing wrong in landed property, and that there is no need to abolish it. One might think it would be palpable to every educated man of our time that the exclusive control of land by people who do not work upon it, and who prevent hundreds and thousands of distressed families making use of it, is an action every whit as wicked and base as the possession of slaves; yet we see aristocrats, supposed to be educated and refined, English, Austrian, Prussian, Russian, who profit by this cruel and base right, and who are not only not ashamed, but proud of it.

Religion blesses such possession, and the science of political economy proves that it must exist for the greatest welfare of mankind. It is Henry George's merit that he not only exploded all the sophism whereby religion and science justify landed property, and pressed the question to the farthest proof, which forced all who had not stopped their ears to acknowledge the unlawfulness of ownerships in land, but also that he was the first to indicate a possibility of solution for the question. He was the first to give a simple, straightforward answer to the usual excuses made by the enemies of all progress, which affirm that the demands of progress are illusions, impracticable, inapplicable.

The method of Henry George destroys this excuse by so putting the question that by to-morrow committees might be appointed to examine and deliberate on his scheme and its transformation into law. In Russia, for instance, the inquiry as to the means for the ransom of land, or its gratuitous confiscation for nationalisation, might be begun to-morrow, and solved, with certain restrictions, as thirty-three years ago the question of liberating the peasants was solved. To humanity the indispensableness of this reform is demonstrated, and its feasibleness is proved (emendations, alterations in the single tax system may be required, but the fundamental idea is a possibility); and therefore humanity cannot but do that which their reason demands. It is only necessary, in order that this idea may become public opinion, that it should be spread and explained precisely as you are doing, in which cause I sympathise with you with all my heart, and wish you success.

II.

The scheme of Henry George is as follows:—The advantage and profit from the use of land is not everywhere the same, since the more fertile, convenient portions, adjoining populous districts, will always attract many who wish to possess them; and so much the more as these portions are better and more suitable, they ought to be appraised according to their advantages; the better, dearer; the worse, cheaper; the worst, cheapest of all.

Whereas the land which attracts but few should not be appraised at all, but conceded without payment to those who are willing to cultivate it by their own manual labour. According to such a valuation, convenient plough land in the government of Toula, for example, would be valued at about five or six roubles the dessyatin (about two and three-quarter acres); market garden land near villages at ten roubles; the same, but liable to spring floods, fifteen roubles, and so on. In towns the valuation would be from one hundred to five hundred roubles the dessyatin; and in Moscow and Petersburg, in go-ahead places, and about the harbours of navigable rivers, several thousands or tens of thousands of roubles the dessyatin.

When all the land in the country has been thus appraised, Henry George pro-

poses to pass a law declaring that all the
land, from such a year and date, shall
belong no longer to any separate individual,
but to the whole country, to the whole
nation; and that thereafter everyone who
possesses land must gradually pay to the
State, that is, to the whole nation, the
price at which it has been appraised.

This payment must be expended on all
the public needs of the State, so that it
will take the place of every kind of mone-
tary imposition, both local and national
—the custom house, etc.

According to this scheme it would
follow that a landowner, who was at
present in possession of two thousand
dessyatins, would continue to own them,
but would have to pay for them into the
treasury, here in Toula, between twelve
and fifteen thousand roubles a year,
because hereabouts the best land for agricultural and building purposes would be
included; and no large landowner would
be able to bear the strain of such a payment, and would be obliged to give up the
land. Whereas our Toula peasant would
have to pay about two roubles less for
each dessyatin of the same ground than he
does at present, would always have avail-
able land around him which he could hire
for five or six roubles, and, in addition,
would not only have no other taxes to pay,
but would receive all Russian and foreign
articles which he needs without imposts.
In towns the owners of houses and manu-
factories can continue to possess their

property, but will have to pay for the land they occupy, according to its valuation, into the common treasury.

The advantage of such a system will be—

1. That no one will be deprived of the possibility of using land.

2. That idle men, possessing land, and forcing others to work for them in return for the use of the land, will cease to exist.

3. That the land will be in the hands of those who work it and not of those who do not.

4. That the people being able to work on the land will cease to enslave themselves as labourers in mills and factories, and as servants in towns; and will disperse themselves about the country.

5. That there will be no longer any overseers and tax collectors in factories, mills, stores, and custom houses, but only collectors of payment for the land, which it is impossible to steal, and from which taxes may be most easily collected.

6, and chiefly. That those who do not labour will be freed from the sin of profiting by the labours of others (in doing which they are often not to blame, being from childhood educated in idleness, and not knowing how to work); and from the still greater sin of every kind of falsehood and excuse to shift the blame from themselves; and that those who do labour will be delivered from the temptation and sin of envy, condemnation of others, and exasperation against those who do not work; and thus will disappear one of the causes of dissension between man and man.

(First published in *The New Age*. Revised from original.)

On Communal Life

(*From a Letter to a Friend*)

It is quite true, as you say in your article, and H—— in his, that Christian life is quite impossible in the present unchristian organisation of society. The contradiction between his surroundings and his convictions is very painful for a man who is sincere in his Christian faith, and therefore the organisation of communities seems to such a man the only means of delivering himself from these contradictions.

But this is an illusion. Every community is a small island in the midst of an ocean of unchristian conditions of life, so that the Christian relations exist only between the members of the colony; while outside they must remain unchristian, otherwise the colony could not exist for one moment. And therefore to live in a community cannot save a Christian from the contradiction between his conscience and his life.

I do not mean to say that I do not approve of the organisation of communities such as your commonwealth, or that I do not think them good things. On the contrary, I approve of them with all my heart, and am very interested in your commonwealth, and wish it the greatest success.

I think that every man who *can* free himself from the conditions of worldly life without breaking the ties of love,—love, the main principle, in the name of which he is seeking new forms of life,—I think such a man not only must, but will naturally join people who have the same beliefs, and who try to live up to them. If I were free I would immediately, even at my age, join such a colony.

I only wished to say that the mere forming of communities is not a solution of the Christian problem, but is only one of the means for its solution. The revolution that is going on for the attainment of the Christian ideal is so enormous, our life is so different from what it ought to be, that for the perfect success of this revolution, for the concordance of conscience and life is needed the work of all men—men living in communities, as well as men of the world living in the most different conditions. This ideal is not so quickly and so simply attained as we think and wish, and the ideal will be attained only when every man in the whole world will say: "Why should I sell my services and buy yours? If mine are greater than yours, I owe them to you." For, if there be in the whole world one man who does not think and act by this principle, and who will appropriate and keep by violence what he can take from others, no man can live a true Christian life, whether it be in a community or outside it. We cannot be / saved separately, we must be saved altogether. And this can be attained only through the modification of the conception of life, *i.e.* the faith of all men. And to this end we must work all together—men living in the world, as well as men living in communities.

We must all of us remember that we are messengers from the great King, the God of love, with the message of unity and love amongst all living beings. And, therefore, we must not for a minute forget our mission, and may do all that we think useful and agreeable for ourselves, *only* so long as it is not in opposition to our mission, which is to be accomplished not only by words, but by example, and especially by the infection of love.

Please give my respect and love to the colonists, and ask them not to be offended by my giving them advice which may be unnecessary.

I advise them to remember that all material questions, money, implements, even nourishment, the very existence of the colony itself, all these things are of little importance in comparison with the sole object of our life : to preserve love amongst all men with whom we come in contact. If, with the object of keeping the interests of the colony, or of protecting the thrift of it, you must quarrel with a friend or with a stranger, must excite ill-feeling in somebody, it is better to give up everything than to act against love.

And let your friends not dread that the strict following of this principle will destroy the practical work. Even the practical work will flourish, not as we expect it, but in its own way, only if we are strictly following the law of love; and will perish if we act in opposition to it.

PRINTED BY
MORRISON AND GIBB LIMITED, EDINBURGH